"*Breaking the Cycle* by George Collins is a 911 call that can save your life and those you love from sex addiction, porn obsession, and shame. Honest, stark, hard-hitting and yet hopeful, Collins lays out the steps required to wrestle self-control back from your sexually compulsive impulses. In your darkest time, *Breaking the Cycle* brings the light you are looking for!"

> —Don Elium, MFT, adjunct faculty at John F. Kennedy University and author of *Raising a Son*

"Prior to reading this book, I had been acting out my sexually compulsive behaviors for forty years. Each chapter is filled with specific experiences and emotions that I have struggled with in the past. As a result of the techniques described in this book, my addiction has faded away."

> —Ralph, sex addict in recovery in Rhode Island

"This book offers a raw look into the world of sex addicts. George Collins' courageous self-revelation of his own sex addiction has helped hundreds of men and women to find what is essential for rehabilitation inside themselves. His 'I'll pay you to just be honest' conversation with the sex worker and client was itself worth the cost of the book!"

> —Don L. Mathews, MFT, director of the Impulse Treatment Center

"This is gripping stuff, and a real page-turner of a book. The real-life stories have the ring of truth, and the dialogue is unmistakably real. The use of trenchant, memorable lines, like, 'you can't get enough of what won't satisfy you,' really get the message across."

— Bob, sex addict in recovery in California

"This book draws on over twenty-five years of Collins' work with hundreds of clients. The book is practical and clearly presents excellent exercises that can help readers progressively free themselves from the grip of sexual compulsions. Most of all, it provides hope."

—Mark Robinett, MFT, therapist in San
Francisco and San Rafael, CA

Collins' take on the mental obsession leading to physical addiction and subsequent negative consequence is pure poetry for the troubled romantic soul. Even if you are NOT an addict, you will find this book a useful GPS to navigate new neighborhoods of abnormal thinking in people you know or will encounter someday. On a personal note, I am honored to be mentioned and I am grateful he didn't abbreviate First Thought Wrong even one time. Thank you, George, for taking First Thought Wrong from sexual to helpful, hopeful and safe."

—Mark Lundholm, internationally recognized stand-up
comedian and creator of *The Recovery Board
Game* and the DVD series *Humor in Treatment*

Breaking the Cycle

Free Yourself from Sex Addiction, Porn Obsession, and Shame

GEORGE N. COLLINS, MA
with ANDREW ADLEMAN, MA

New Harbinger Publications, Inc.

Publisher's Note

This publication is designed to provide accurate and authoritative information in regard to the subject matter covered. It is sold with the understanding that the publisher is not engaged in rendering psychological, financial, legal, or other professional services. If expert assistance or counseling is needed, the services of a competent professional should be sought.

Distributed in Canada by Raincoast Books

Copyright © 2010 by George N. Collins
New Harbinger Publications, Inc.
5674 Shattuck Avenue
Oakland, CA 94609
www.newharbinger.com

Author photograph by James Fidelibus
Acquired by Jess O'Brien
Cover design by Amy Shoup

Library of Congress Cataloging-in-Publication Data

Collins, George N.
    Breaking the cycle : free yourself from sex addiction, porn obsession, and shame / George N. Collins with Andrew Adleman.
        p. cm.
    Includes bibliographical references.
    ISBN 978-1-60882-083-2 (pbk.) -- ISBN 978-1-60882-084-9 (pdf e-book) -- ISBN 978-1-60882-085-6 (epub)
    1. Sex addiction. 2. Sex addiction--Treatment. I. Adleman, Andrew. II. Title.
    RC560.S43C65 2011
    616.85'833--dc23

                        2011023262

12 11 10   10 9 8 7 6 5 4 3 2 1   First printing

To my wife, Paldrom, who has brought light and truth to my life.

Contents

Acknowledgments

Firstly, thank you to Recovery, Incorporated which, early on, was a literal lifesaver in helping me prepare to face my addiction. Much appreciation goes to my brother, Charles, and my sister, Denise, who each encouraged me to pursue my education. I also want to acknowledge my cosponsors Mike, Roger, and Rob, as well as Don Mathews, MFT, all of whom were a great help through my early recovery. I am grateful for the wisdom of Ramana Maharshi, which has been a positive influence on my counseling practice. I want to thank my colleagues at Compulsion Solutions—Greg Brian, James Gallegos, and Faye Reitman—for their dedication and hard work. Thank you to my cowriter and friend, Andrew Adleman, for translating my ramblings and ideas into readable text. Thanks also to the staff at New Harbinger Publications for their gracious guidance with the editing and publishing process. And, finally, thank you to all my current and former clients, who continue to be my greatest teachers.

Introduction

Bob nervously watched the big TV as the seconds counted down to Super Bowl halftime and the football teams left the field. "It's halftime," said Bob to his wife. "I'm going to make a quick business call."

Bob got up from the couch and walked down the hall to his oak-paneled office. Already lost in his addiction, his mind was cluttered with images regarding what he was going to see on the computer screen. Bob was in such a hurry that he quickly shut the door behind him, neglecting to turn the lock. He rushed to his large desk, sat in the luxury leather office chair, and flipped on the thirty-inch monitor. Out the window was an incredible view of the mountains, but Bob didn't see it. His eyes saw only the computer screen as his fingers quickly reached the website he wanted. Having been there so many times, he was able to quickly sign in and navigate to a specific video. Finally, it started.

Bob pulled down his sweat pants so his genitals were exposed. He moved into just the right position in the chair and began his very familiar ritual of masturbating to these types of images and videos. He had seen hundreds over the years. His wife had caught him three times, and the last time she had said that the next time would be "it" for their marriage. Bob had tried to stop, but didn't. So here he was again, thinking of nothing else but the images on the screen.

On his monitor was a video of a young woman being forcefully held down and sodomized by three men in masks. Although Bob had never done this in real life (and most likely never would), watching domination is what got him the most turned on. His right hand in motion, Bob got more and more excited. He was lost. Gone. And he didn't hear the door start to open. Bob usually double-checked the lock on the door, and, like most addicts, he lived with the illusion that he would never slip up. But this time he was in such a hurry to do what he needed and get back to the game that he thought the door was locked. It wasn't.

Just as Bob began to climax, his ten-year-old daughter opened the door and stood there, motionless, shocked, and terrified at the sight of her father ejaculating to the horrendous images on the computer monitor. Melanie ran screaming to her mother.

Bob no longer lives at that house.

His wife had warned him that he was down to his last chance, and her attorney showed no mercy toward Bob—not after what Melanie had seen.

Four years later, his daughter was still in therapy. Bob had only supervised visits with her. A glum-faced Child Protection Services official needed to be present at all times. Bob's ex-wife was still so angry that she communicated with Bob only through her attorney.

■ How Bob Changed His Life

In many ways, Bob was considered a good father and what many people thought of as a nice guy. But he was caught by his compulsion. The Internet had him by the balls. He just could not stop. Yet, for men like Bob, there is a way to break the stranglehold of the compulsion. The incident that occurred when his daughter walked into his home office finally convinced Bob to get counseling. He had "hit bottom." Alone in the motel room where he was forced to live, Bob finally called me.

Now he has gone through treatment and is forging a new life—a life free of porn and moving in the direction of true intimacy with a real woman in his life. It was not easy. Bob wasn't a bad guy at heart, and he went through a great deal of despair and horror at his own behavior. In a technique that you will learn in this book, I guided Bob through the process of understanding that he was more than his mind, his thoughts, or his addiction. He was so much more.

In the beginning of our work together, I asked him to bookend his days by calling me in the morning and at night to report on his feelings and actions. I wanted him to be able to hold himself accountable and to get support from me if he needed it. After all, I know what being in the grip of the compulsion is like. I've been there myself. Bob could tell that I really did care that he got well.

Bob's Success

Bob's progress took a lot of time and work, including practicing the techniques briefly described below. Eventually, Bob began to associate porn with suffering, not bliss. After more time passed, Bob began dating a woman in CoDA (Codependents Anonymous) recovery. He learned about true intimacy and true happiness. Without the pull of porn, Bob had even more time and energy to devote to his business. His income has increased, and he's begun to donate to recovery causes. This does not in any way excuse his selfish, addictive behavior. Yet it does show that he has begun the process of forgiveness and redemption.

Bob learned all the techniques that I'll be teaching you in this book. What follows now are brief descriptions of just a few of those techniques, which will be explained in detail in later chapters. In each chapter I'll also present real-life examples of how the techniques work, though the names and some of the details in the examples have been changed to protect privacy.

Is This Book For You?

Patrick Carnes, author of many excellent books including *Out of the Shadows: Understanding Sexual Addiction* (the breakthrough book on sexually compulsive behavior), defines *sexual addiction* as any sex-related compulsion that interferes with normal living and causes severe stress to family, friends, loved ones, and one's work environment. Sex addicts frequently make sex a priority over relationships and work (Carnes 2001). If you're suffering from any form of sexual compulsivity—using porn, prostitutes, chat rooms, phone sex, and so on—then this book is for you. By following the steps in the book, you can finally break free of the wretched regressive story, the childish behavior, and the narcissistic urges. Your life will change for the better. In addition to men with a wide range of sexually addictive behavior, my clients have included a large number of women, many of whom were addicted to sex-oriented chat rooms, relationships, and love. My clients have also included many gay men and women who have had a range of sexually addictive behaviors, usually with a tendency toward cruising and having anonymous sex.

The techniques I use work for almost everyone, and this book could've been written with examples for every possible sexual type and variation of addict, whether straight, gay, male, or female. However, in the interest of simplicity and the book being concise and easy to read, most of it is written in a way that addresses heterosexual males. Obviously, you might be a woman, or gay, or transsexual. If you're not a heterosexual male, I encourage you to make the appropriate adjustments in wording for your individual needs and addictive behaviors. In addition, if you are buying this book for someone else but also plan to possibly read it yourself, you can adjust the wording to fit your situation.

Techniques That Interfere with Your Addictive Impulses

One technique about listening to your addiction is called "Turning On the Lights in Your Amphitheater." You will learn to review and monitor your own internal amphitheater of protagonists and helpers. Rather than having a number of inner voices or subpersonalities all trying to talk at once, you can choose one subpersonality and/or complex that you would like to have speak. Your addict might not talk right away but, believe me, there is a part of you in there that wants to talk. From there, you can begin to create a new internal subpersonality that will be your champion and can help you refuse to act out. This sounds more complicated than it is, but it's fully explained in an easy-to-follow way in chapter 2.

Chapter 5 includes a section called "What's Always True?" This section introduces a technique that helps you drop down into your essential self, becoming aware, just for a moment, of the connectedness you experience in your most peaceful moments. Focusing on what is always true will help you start to be who you truly are rather than who you think yourself to be. Typically, much of your thinking comes from your experience of what other people have told you rather than from your true essence.

Chapter 9 has a description of my experience with "Blue Sky and High Heels," which is a way for you to know what to do when sexually compulsive thought patterns enter your mind. For example, suppose you're walking around and, in a flash that's faster than what I call "clock time," you smell perfume and you want to have sex—with anybody. Perfume equals sex. It's a story you've made up in your mind, and you don't know when or how it's going to hit you. The Blue Sky and High Heels technique provides a way to be aware that this will happen and teaches you how to be prepared to deal with your impulses.

Another technique that interferes with addictive impulses is what I call "The Red Light Guy," which is covered in depth in chapter 11. It's a fun technique to convert sexual energy into positive adult behavior and thinking. In chapter 12, you'll find "First Thought Wrong," which is about learning to question the voice of your addict. The "How Good Can You Stand It?" technique in chapter 14 is an affirmation that can change your life for the better.

These are only a sample of the techniques for overcoming sexual addiction that you will discover in this book. Regardless of your sex, gender, sexual orientation, or sexual desires, a sex addict's individual behavioral compulsions have a seemingly unshakeable grip that can end up ruining their lives. But there are many variations of Bob's story, and you too can break free of the shackles of sex addiction. Although, in my case, the type of porn was not what Bob would have chosen, the impact on my own marriage—no, make that *marriages*—was the same.

How I Changed My Life

Many years ago, I was a sex addict living in the grip of my compulsion. I was down and almost out. My second wife had left me because I was depressed from too much porn—videos, seedy the-aters, and magazines—and I had no clue how to be intimate with a real, live, loving woman. I had a great job with a good salary, and it was fun work. But without my lovely wife, I just felt hope-less. This was the second wife I'd lost to porn and the underlying issues. I got so depressed that I took an overdose of tranquilizers. I felt that hopeless. Luckily, my mother, who lived in another state, knew I was in terrible shape. When I didn't answer my phone, she called the local police. They took me to the hospital, where I woke up in the ICU.

From that lowest of low points, I began to overcome my addiction by attending self-help and recovery groups. I then went on to earn a master's degree in counseling psychology at John F. Kennedy University so I could help others, which I've been doing successfully since 1995. I also met and married a wonderful woman with whom I am finally able to experience true intimacy.

This book can show you the way out of your addiction and into real intimacy with another human being. In addition, without a sexual addiction, you'll have more energy and time to make friends and enjoy hobbies. It's also very likely that you'll increase your income. If I can do it, so can you. It's the difference between being enslaved and being free. Which do you choose?

You Always Have a Choice

If you choose to be free of the compulsion that you are allowing to run your life, I will show you the steps you can take to be free of your impulses. In addition, you can learn to experience true closeness and intimacy with another.

When helping my clients, I use the techniques I mentioned earlier, along with other processes you'll learn about in the follow-ing chapters. These methods have stood the test of time. Some are my own discoveries, while others I learned in my studies, from 12-step programs, or from several wonderful mentors. Keep in mind, I was a sex addict and I got better, which means I have a deep understanding of what works and what doesn't. In this book, you will learn the ways that I and many others became sane. When I say "sane," I mean no longer being driven primarily by the desire to act out sexually. This is not to say that you will eliminate sex from your life or even from your thoughts. Of course it's normal and healthy to have sexual desire and to experience sex. But it is neither normal nor healthy for sexual desire to become all consuming. Sexual desire should be a part of a larger approach you have to life. The goal is balance. Interactions with partners should be about love and intimacy in addition to being about sex.

Let me simply describe something that took me a long time to learn and which you will probably not absorb just by reading this paragraph: *I am not my addiction. You are not your addiction.* No one has to be defined by his or her addictive behavior. I am infinitely more than my addiction, and so are you.

Your addiction is now all consuming—and possibly all defeating. It is probably ruining your life. But you are so much more than your addiction. And when you realize this, you can put your addiction into perspective and begin to deal with it. Again: you have a choice.

Or maybe you are one of those who will procrastinate until it seems you don't have a choice. But, once more, the truth is: *you always have a choice.* In chapter 10, I explain that concept in depth. For now, let's just say that this book shows you how to choose to break free from sexual compulsions, how to stick with that choice to be free, and how to move on to a more fulfilling life.

My promise to you is that you can get free so that you're not out of control and you can experience intimacy. But to fulfill my part of the bargain, I need to repeat myself so that the concepts get through to you. I'm not saying you have a thick skull. It's just that the part of you that is addicted ("your addict") may be resistant and try to pull you off the path to freedom. (Remember all the times that you've tried to stop on your own?)

When that happens, and you're pulled off the path, another crucial thing to remember is this: *you are not your mind.* In other words, you are not who you *think* you are or who your addict keeps telling you you are. You've been living in reaction to your history. We all do, and this is mostly okay. An exception is when living in reaction to your past results in sexually compulsive behavior. If you realize the essential truth that you are not your mind, you can experience actually making choices in the moment. That means you can live without your stories telling you that you can't be successful or have real intimacy, and living without those negative stories can mean that you no longer have to act out sexually. When everything you do is fresh and you're no longer living in reaction to your history, there are no preconceived notions, no story. Your life will be different. That's what Bob ultimately did. But he waited until he had hit bottom and lost his home, lost his marriage, and severely limited his right to see his own child.

Are you going to wait until you hit bottom? Will you wait until you feel you have no choice? Or are you going to make that choice now? If you're not ready to change your life, then don't buy this book.

How Difficult Is It?

It's difficult. I won't bullshit you. And you can do it. This book offers a condensed version of what happens in sessions with clients, either in person or over the phone. My associates and I at Compulsion Solutions treat people from all over the United States, as well as from the rest of the world. The book will guide you, step by step, through processes that have been proven to work.

I was addicted to porn, peep shows, and strip clubs. I've counseled clients who have done almost anything imaginable. What I describe in the following chapters are the treatment techniques I use with clients, but which I first used on myself. They helped me not only to become free of sexually compulsive behavior but also to realize that I'm not my addiction—that I'm not even my "mind," nor am I all the stories I've told myself about myself. I am infinitely more than my addiction, and today I enjoy a level of consciousness far beyond the memories, projections, and associated feelings of what I used to call my life.

You can have this too. Because you and I are not that different.

If you work through this book, you'll know what I'm talking about. Really. You might not believe me yet. The truth is that it's actually *fun* to be conscious and present (most of the time) instead of being lost in a life of quiet desperation.

Your path to freedom starts, as mine did, with the realization that you've lost control around sex. You begin by acknowledging that you're acting regressively (like a twelve- to fifteen-year-old, at best), and that you're probably a mature man in most ways, *but* you don't understand intimacy and have confused intimacy with sexual activity.

Also—and this is crucial—you are beginning to realize that you can't get enough of what won't satisfy you! Objectifying and sexualizing people is a never-ending, negative process that yields a few minutes of excitement, a brief orgasm, then hours, days, weeks, months, and years of fear, pain, shame, self-doubt, self-criticism, judgment, and anger. Doing the work in this book will help free you from the shackles of your own negative sexual story.

How do I know? Because I did it and have seen hundreds of clients—like you—break free of sexual compulsions. It will take courage to do the assignments in this book. I can vouch for that.

However, this could be your rite of passage into true manhood, free of your old compulsive sexual desires.

It's worth the discomfort. Try to work the steps or techniques in sequence as they are presented in the book. Some parts may be easier for you than others. The chapters are in the order they're in because, in my many years of counseling experience, this sequence has proven the most effective at freeing individuals from the grip of their sexual compulsions. I know it's a cliché now, but "Just do it!" I adopted that saying early on, and it's helped me immensely.

When you're having a difficult time, remember that I didn't just read about this in a psychology book. I *lived* the life of a sex addict. I took the worst thing that ever happened to me and made it into a thriving business—because the treatment processes I use work. You can take the energy you're expending on addictive behavior and channel it into a more satisfying career, intimacy and better relationships with a partner and with your family and dear friends, and meaningful activities. In other words, if you follow the steps in this book, you'll actually get a life.

CHAPTER 1

Are You Under the Spell of Sex Addiction?

Take a good look at your own behavior. Is there someone who might discover what you're up to and say, "This is your last chance"? Could there be a problem with the law, such as being arrested with a prostitute? Could a spouse or child discover the porn on your computer? Could your wife find you masturbating to porn in front of the TV (where your children might also see you)? What would need to happen to make you decide you have a problem? Who would need to find out? Think about it. It happens to people like you every day, and it can happen to you. *Just think about it.*

Are You a Train Wreck Waiting to Happen?

Would it take something like what happened to Bob when his young daughter walked in on him? Or could you "hit bottom" when it looks as though you're doing okay and you're still maintaining, by realizing your life could totally self-destruct at any moment? Howard is a good example of someone who took action before his life could become a train wreck.

■ *Howard and the Working Girl*

Driving his brand new, shiny black Lexus sedan, Howard turned off Highway 580 and guided his car the few blocks to San Pablo Avenue in Oakland, California. At that time, San Pablo Avenue was a grungy thoroughfare, parts of which were littered with used drug needles and empty liquor bottles. It has since been cleaned up, although many areas are still run down. At that time, the notable "attraction" of San Pablo Avenue was that it was known as an area where prostitutes solicited customers while walking the unswept sidewalks or leaning into cars from dirty curbsides.

A heavyset man with curly red hair and very pale skin, Howard had achieved financial success as a programmer for a major software company. He frequently traveled and had no clue about how to date. Lately, Howard's job had been more and more affected by his compulsion to "visit" working girls. As a result, his job performance was suffering and his social life, which had never been great, was basically going down the tubes.

But this time, as Howard slowed the Lexus to get a good look at the "girls" on the street, there was a difference. Howard knew he was in trouble, and he didn't want to lose the life he had worked so hard to build. He had called me and had started sex-addiction counseling. It was going well. So why was he once again cruising San Pablo Avenue? Because I had asked him to.

What? His sex addiction counselor had asked him to look for a prostitute?

Yes! Except this time his counselor—me—was sitting comfortably in the back seat of the Lexus. I frequently give clients assignments and, when I think it's needed or would be effective, the client's counseling session might be a field trip, with me along for moral support or merely to stir things up. In Howard's case, I wanted to provoke a serious change in his initial interaction with a prostitute.

Howard's assignment—with me in the back seat of the Lexus—was to go to San Pablo Avenue and pick up a prostitute. But this time it wasn't about getting sex. Rather, Howard was working to break the stranglehold of his sexual addiction. And he was nervous about what was going to happen. After several minutes of procrastination, Howard pulled the car up next to the type of woman he habitually hired.

Although she was probably about twenty-two, she looked older, and tired, and her teased blonde hair was not properly combed. Her low-cut, pink blouse and short, tight-fitting skirt showed several light stains. When she smiled, her yellowing teeth were chipped. Her breath was strong, and it was clear she was not taking the best care of herself.

"What you looking for today, Hon?" she asked Howard.

"I, um," Howard stammered uncomfortably. "How much do you charge to just, um, party?"

She named a price and Howard glanced back at me. I leaned forward in the seat so she could see me.

"So is this a twofer?" she asked.

"No," I said. "I'm a sex-addiction counselor."

"What? What is this?" she said, alarmed.

Howard gripped the steering wheel, his knuckles white and his hands sweaty.

"He'll pay you for your time," I said. "No problem."

While I continued to sit in the back seat, I motioned for the woman to get in the front.

She opened the door and sat in the passenger's seat, saying, "You're definitely going to pay?"

Howard nodded and opened his wallet so she could see that he had the cash. She visibly relaxed, and I could tell she would be happy to cooperate in any way possible.

As Howard drove to a nearby semi-secluded area, I said, "My client is addicted to prostitutes."

"That's what I'm here for," she said, with a cheery smile.

Howard glanced at her face, then at her breasts. He was sweating even more now.

"He wants to have sex with you. Do you want to have sex with him?" I asked.

"Sure. So long as he pays me," she said.

"But do you really want to have sex with him?" I asked, keeping my voice low and gentle.

"What do you mean?" she asked, even though she knew exactly what I meant.

"I mean, do you enjoy it? Do you enjoy being with men like this man?"

The artificial smile on her face faltered. I knew I'd hit a nerve. She was off her game now. Flustered, she tried to regain her composure and angrily set her jaw. I have a lot of practice at providing a safe environment for people to open up, though I don't typically do this on the street anymore. It could be dangerous. Her pimp could have been following us or she could have had a knife. My intention at the time was to help

Howard achieve a breakthrough and see that the prostitute
was a real human being.

"Do you really love to have sex with men you don't
know?" I asked again, keeping my voice gentle yet forceful.
"It's okay to say how you really feel. Right now you're getting
paid for not having sex."

She glanced at me, then at Howard, who was trying not
to look at her body but couldn't help himself. She glared at
him now, her anger rising.

"It's okay," I said again. "It would be very helpful for my
client to hear the truth."

"The truth? You really want the truth?" She hesitated. It
wasn't easy for her to speak. She shook her head.

I nodded, encouraging her with my eyes to continue.
Although my goal was to intervene in the situation so my
client would have a very different and new street experience,
I also felt compassion for the woman. (Prostitutes occasionally
call my office for help, and I refer them to appropriate
organizations.) When she realized neither Howard nor I
wanted anything sexual from her and she was going to get
paid anyway, she dropped her hard-edged veneer, at least a
little, and she began unburdening herself. She also must have
sensed that I cared enough to do what must have seemed
like a crazy intervention. Maybe she was having a bad day.
Gradually, as we talked for a while, her anger came spilling
out and she got to her story about herself and prostitution.

"Okay, okay, I guess the truth is—the truth is I don't really
like men all that much," she said, her voice barely audible.

She glared at Howard again and folded her arms across
her chest.

"Can you say that again, louder?" I asked. Although it
seems improbable that a sex worker would open up, I had
been making interventions similar to this for years. I also had

been receiving several calls a week from sex workers wanting to leave the trade. This had given me more experience in talking with them and in encouraging them to speak candidly.

"I fucking hate men! Okay?!" she said vehemently now. "My father was a total asshole. The things he did. Motherfucker!" There were tears in her eyes and she couldn't stop them. She quickly patted her face, not wanting to smear her thick makeup.

Howard was inches from her, taking this all in. Sweat dripped from his forehead.

"He beat me and my sisters!" she continued. "And he fucked us. All of us. Treated us like, like things to be used and thrown away. Men are such assholes!"

She glared at me, shaking her head. But our eyes met and she knew I understood something about who she was and what she'd been through. She could tell that I wasn't seeing her as an object, but as a person—a woman in pain. Howard could also see it. I could tell that, by this time, he was no longer wanting sex and had received his lesson, which was to permanently disrupt his addictive behavior. I told Howard to pay her the money and drop her off back on San Pablo Avenue.

That experience with the prostitute changed Howard. He was different. I won't kid you and say his urges totally stopped at that moment. That took a lot more work. But that moment clarified in the deepest part of Howard that his sexually compulsive behavior was something he could no longer tolerate. It triggered an immense amount of empathy and loving-kindness for himself as well as for the women he had hired for sex. After that experience, all prostitutes looked different. It was the catalyst for his solid launch into recovery. Whenever he had the compulsion to hire a prostitute, our brief visit to San Pablo Avenue jumped into his mind and he could no longer unconsciously give in to his addiction.

As a side note, I gave the prostitute my business card. She called me several weeks later, and I referred her to an organization that assists prostitutes in leaving sex work and finding other careers.

After Howard made the decision to change his life, he went through weeks of discovery about himself and his life history (which I call his story). He learned techniques to deal with his impulses and began healing his original emotional wound. This meant that he began coming to terms with unresolved emotional experiences from childhood that result in coping behaviors that can contribute to a tendency to act out sexually. After several years of dedicated counseling work, Howard was married. I was invited to the wedding and stood at the back of the church. As Howard walked down the aisle, we exchanged glances and he nodded at me in thanks.

Again, I don't want to sugarcoat the process of change. It was difficult and time consuming for Howard and, even after his marriage, our work together continued. And, like Howard, you can change. What this book can do for you is to teach you how to deal with your addiction, so your addiction is no longer running your life. One way to do that is by starting at the beginning.

You Calling Me a Sex Addict?

No one wants to admit that he's addicted. Yet we all have impulses or compulsions that we'd rather not have. The difference between addiction and compulsion is really just language. Every one of us would have to say that we have an addiction to something. We all have an addiction to certain beliefs. If you're reading this book, you're probably a certain kind of addict—a sex addict. Or you may prefer the word "compulsion" to "addiction." I know I do. In fact, if you go by the dictionary definition, compulsion fits better than addiction, because compulsion is a need to *do* something. In defining sex addiction, psychologist and author Patrick Carnes uses the words "sexually compulsive behavior" (Carnes 2010). Unlike the word "compulsion," the word "addiction" has a stigma attached to it. Even though sexual addiction may more accurately be labeled a compulsion, the word addiction is commonly used, as well as the word "addict." Therefore, this book will use both addiction and compulsion.

Patrick Carnes wrote an apt description of the addict's behavior: "The addict substitutes a sick relationship to an event or a process for a healthy relationship with others. The addict's relationship with a mood-altering experience becomes central to his life" (Carnes 2001, 14).

For me, acknowledging that I was an addict was a matter of realizing the truth of a great truism that I may mention often in this book: *You can't get enough of what won't satisfy you.* If you keep trying to get that "something"—whatever it is that you get over and over while remaining unsatisfied—you're an addict. But where do these compulsions originate?

Coping Strategies for Uncomfortable Feelings

You are a product of your early environment. If your home was weighed down with alcohol, drugs, fighting, divorce, changing environments (frequent moves), porn, overparenting, lack of parenting, or abandonment, then these situations most likely led to an imbalance in your life. You probably developed coping strategies to deal with your fear, shame, pain, self-doubt, judgment, criticism, and anger. Maybe you adapted and socialized so that you were connected with others. Or, maybe you felt isolated, in which case your coping strategy may have been addiction or, more specifically, sexually compulsive behavior.

Since sex is going to be on the mind of a young guy and it feels good, you may have found ways to express your angst through compulsive masturbation, peeping, inappropriate touching, or some other variation of compulsive behavior. Of course, since on the surface most sex in our culture is not spoken about openly, you had to keep it a secret.

In a 12-step recovery program, there is a saying: "We're only as sick as our secrets." Very true. But who can you tell? Probably no one. And, like most of us, you probably didn't get "the talk" from your parents. Not a talk that made any sense anyway. You probably heard the locker room bragging of sexual conquests and how much pussy this or that man claimed to be getting. You may have developed "relationships" with pictures, negative sexual actions, or inappropriate partners. You probably started to misinterpret sex, considering it to be the same experience as true intimacy. The result may have been that your addictive behavior felt soothing rather than disgusting and stupid.

Who Becomes a Sex Addict?

Almost anybody who suffered as a child can become a sex addict. Some circumstances might push an individual more in the direction of healing childhood wounds rather than making do with simply coping. Other conditions might lead to beliefs about himself that require a coping strategy. In general, we establish patterns of behavior. For some people, the coping could be eating. For others, it becomes sex addiction. Can you think of your sex addiction as a coping strategy? Perhaps, as a child, you experienced a certain stimulation or overstimulation. You might have discovered your dad's porn or played doctor with a neighbor girl. This early sexual stimulation typically felt nice. As soon as a young child develops the ability to be stimulated, whether through his ears, eyes, nose, hands, or genitals, he naturally becomes interested in revisiting that stimulation and the resultant good feeling. For example, when a boy misbehaves and is sent to his room, one way of coping with feeling bad is to self-soothe by touching himself sexually.

Other examples of childhood experiences that might lead to sex addiction include a little boy being masturbated by a babysitter, having sex with a primary caregiver or sibling, or spying on his sister or a neighbor; or a mother treating a child like a partner by making the child into what has frequently been referred to in psychology as a "surrogate husband" or, in the case of young girls, a "surrogate wife." An example of such dysfunctional behavior took place in my own life. In my childhood, my mother frequently paid me twenty-five cents to massage her shoulders. "I hate your father," she would say over and over again, often adding, "And you'll always be my little man." One day she asked me to massage her breasts. I was six years old and got a tiny erection. I believed this meant my mother loved me. My mother's behavior continued in ways that resulted in me feeling a deep sense of shame and being pathologically "close" to her.

In psychiatry and psychology, this type of parental behavior has often been called *emotional incest* or *covert incest* (Love and Robinson 1990). It was damaging for me and resulted in an unhealthy view of sex and a distorted view of relationships and intimacy.

After the damaging experiences with my mother, watching peep shows or porn felt much safer to me than interacting with a "real" woman. If I was watching porn or looking at pictures, there was no danger of an incestuous relationship or behavior. There was no danger of a real woman I cared about acting inappropriately in regard to sex, as my mother had done. It was much safer to objectify women and masturbate rather than risk the possibility of intimate connections and hurt feelings.

Years later, as an adult in my late twenties, I was in a booth in a San Francisco peep show parlor (before the Internet was available), and I accidentally dropped my last quarter on the filthy floor. I went ahead and picked it up, all wet and sticky, because I just *had* to watch one more peep. I had started frequenting these shows in my early twenties, and by my late twenties I was an addict.

Confusing Sexual Messages

When we're first discovering our sexuality, it's very powerful. At the same time, our society bombards us with messages about sex that are both stimulating and repressive. It's easy to get stuck right there and not become truly sexually mature. The natural progression in puberty is to be stimulated by the female form—or same-sex bodies, as the case may be—and gradually to discover that intimacy and true connection are superior to making someone into a sexual object. But if you continue objectifying the physical act of sex, it means that you continue to make sex more about compulsive behavior and bodies rather than intimacy.

Changing Your Mind

Many people are stuck at that point, and they frequently confuse sex with intimacy. Part of my counseling typically involves redefining intimacy, and that will be covered in depth throughout this book (with a particular focus in chapter 14). For now, please trust me on this: there's the possibility of a sexual connection so intimate that it can be deep and spectacular. But you will never reach that truly ecstatic state if you're stuck in the mind of an adolescent boy who is interested only in body parts.

My job with clients, and your job when reading this book, is to "grow up the child." Allow yourself to mature. You may always have the wound, but you can be more than the story you tell yourself about that damage. If you can convert that story into something useful, something adult and mature, then the energy around it will shift and your behavior will change. You can then stop acting out addictive behavior.

You can change your mind and the story of who you believe yourself to be. Our minds are like software. We have synaptic grooves—and we can make a new groove. We can have a new reaction to circumstances such as seeing a sexy woman, or man, in the grocery store. It can be different. Really. An early step is to feel the compulsion yet not need to respond to it. What I tell people in counseling is this: "If you have to, chew on a table leg, but don't act out." What that means is that you might be uncomfortable for a while, but you can survive it. You won't die of discomfort. In fact, you'll eventually live better than you ever have before.

In chapter 2, you'll learn how to shed light on the parts of yourself that call out to you to act in a sexually compulsive manner. These are similar to the characters or actors in a story or movie. Every one of us has these immature parts within ourselves that might never grow up. Some people have the idea that they have to wipe the slate clean. But that doesn't happen. What you can do with the immature pieces inside you is to make space for them while limiting their power to persuade you to continue your old, sexually compulsive behavior.

EXERCISE: What Would It Take for You to Hit Bottom?

Take a break from imagining yourself in your usual sexual situations. Instead, imagine yourself getting caught in those sexual situations, or being arrested, or your wife finding out how much money you spend on prostitutes or porn, or anything else that just might cause you to hit bottom. This would be a good time to start taking notes. Write in a journal or a notepad, or just go to your computer and start typing. Find a quiet place and take ten to twenty minutes to answer the following questions:

- How many times have you hit bottom only to relapse and hit bottom all over again?

- In my practice, men often call me only when they're being charged with an illegal sexual offense. Could that happen to you?

- Do you want a high bottom or a low bottom? A *low bottom* is signified by events such as being arrested when soliciting a prostitute and going to jail on porn charges. A *high bottom* is when you hit bottom without having major legal consequences.

Think about it. What would it take for you to hit bottom? And will it be a high or low bottom? Once you've thought about it, ask yourself: What can I do to have a high bottom? Do I even want to change my mind? Maybe there's a voice in your head saying, "No, I don't want to look at my behavior. I don't want to change." The next chapter will explain how to identify these voices of your addiction.

CHAPTER 2

Identifying the Voices
in Your Amphitheater

During the course of my training as a sex-addiction counselor, I wanted to develop a metaphor to explain an aspect of the functioning of the human mind in a way that would be easy and maybe even fun to understand. I created the image of my own personal amphitheater.

Turning On the Lights in Your Personal Amphitheater

I imagined myself in an indoor, circular amphitheater. It was dark, really dark, and I was in the center of the floor of the amphitheater. There were bright spotlights on me, and they followed me wherever I walked. I could tell there were a lot of people up in the stands. They were all observing me. I heard their voices, but the spotlights blinded me when I tried to look up into the crowd.

Then I heard a gruff voice yell out, "Go to the porn site you like best—you know the one—and jerk off! You'll like it!" I was confused, and I squinted to see where the voice came from. But it was dark in the stands and the spotlights blinded me. I cupped my hands and called back, "Who *is* this?" The voice yelled back, "It's none of your business. Just do it!"

I felt like doing what the voice said. I felt compelled. And the compulsion was very strong. Do you know that feeling? Would you like to "see" who is talking in your head?

You've been operating or navigating in the dark. This chapter is about turning on the lights so you can see who is talking in your own amphitheater. These are the different voices in your mind that you hear all day long: "I think I'll get pizza for lunch" or "I need to take a piss" or "I've got to make time to check out that new porn site." It's as if they're voices coming from the dark. The one that's telling you to look at porn or visit a prostitute is the one we're most interested in. Let's call that voice a subpersonality.

In the type of psychology I use in my practice, a subpersonality is a personality mode that kicks in (on a temporary basis) to allow a person to cope with certain types of triggering situations. Psychologist Ken Wilber identifies subpersonalities as "functional self-presentations that navigate particular psychosocial situations" (Wilber, Engler, and Brown 1986, 101). What this means is that if you're lonely, afraid of being rejected, isolated, or whatever the issue is in your case, you may have a subpersonality, or a part of your personality, that tells you that the easiest solution to feeling lonely is to look at porn and masturbate, go to a strip club where the women pretend to like you, or have sex with a prostitute who also pretends to have a good time with you. This subpersonality is an aspect of your addict-self. Subpersonalities can also be positive and do not have to be associated with your addiction.

It's important to note that this book is, of course, not against sex or masturbation. I'm completely in favor of having positive sexual experiences. However, many men experience masturbation and other sexual activities in ways that promote fear, shame, and pain. These people do not know how to stop objectifying and sexualizing women and establish a relationship with a real woman. Their sexual subpersonalities keep them stuck in a negative loop of sexually compulsive behavior. I'll show you a way to break free.

Where Do Your Subpersonalities Originate?

My clients turn on the lights in their amphitheaters and hear their subpersonalities saying things such as, "You're not good enough," "Go to Hooters where the girls won't reject you," "Your older brother is smarter than you," "Your younger brother is better looking," "Don't listen to what other people say—you know that prostitute has a thing for you," and "You know that woman on the chat line would date you if she could."

There are lots of these voices or subpersonalities, and they are usually created as a result of difficult experiences and events that happened in the past, often in childhood. Furthermore, these voices or subpersonalities won't shut up. They go on and on. When did they get started and how can you stop them?

It doesn't matter how "good" your home was. It doesn't matter how nice your parents were. Events occurred that had an impact on you. These stories and your resultant coping strategies are kept in your own amphitheater. They emerge and clamor for your attention when they think it's important. These voices or subpersonalities typically are based on old stories—aspects of your negative history—that are no longer even true. But they still have a great deal of power and they keep you living in reaction to them. They keep you a prisoner of your past. They cause you to feel awkward, sad, angry, afraid, ashamed, judgmental, critical, and so on.

Free Yourself from the Addiction of Compulsive Thinking

As Eckhart Tolle wrote, "This kind of compulsive thinking is actually an addiction. What characterizes an addiction? Quite simply this: you no longer feel that you have the choice to stop. It seems stronger than you. It also gives you a false sense of pleasure, pleasure that invariably turns into pain" (Tolle 1999, 14).

How can you get free of these voices? The first step, which might be clear by now, is to realize that you have your own amphitheater and you can turn on the lights. Illuminating the amphitheater will allow you to see what part of you is talking and demanding that you take an action that could have negative consequences. You can identify your stories and coping strategies from the past that are stored there in the darkness, the voices that prompt you to act out sexually. You can do this by using a simple technique of listening to yourself and creating a dialogue.

If you keep the lights on in your amphitheater and a situation arises in which you hear a voice encouraging you to act out sexually, telling you that you'll feel better, making excuses, or even calling you a wuss, you can talk back to it. These voices and your behaviors feel automatic, but they're not. It's *your* amphitheater. It's happening within you. You have the power of the light switch. You can turn on the lights and see who is talking.

Maybe it's not an amphitheater in your case. You can make it a TV studio or a stadium. It doesn't matter if it's a circus tent. What matters is that you hear your subpersonalities talking. Again, the point of this chapter is to realize that you're in the dark and that you're going to turn on the lights. Do you have more choices in a dark room or a well-lit room?

■ *Zane Turns on the Lights in His Amphitheater*

In Zane's case, it was the painfulness of his isolation that finally pushed him to confront his addict self. Zane turned on the lights in his amphitheater and talked with a subpersonality of his addict-self. Remember, there may be many subpersonalities, though often there is one that is more insistent than the others.

Zane had played basketball in high school, so he imagined that he was in a dark gymnasium with people in the stands. But it was too dark to see anyone. As he walked around the floor of the gym, he could see hardly anything. A bright spotlight followed him everywhere he walked. He felt very alone, yet he knew there were people in the stands watching him. He felt foolish, but he kept on trying. This dialogue was the result of his inner conversation with one of his subpersonalities, called Addict-Self:

Zane: C'mon, I know you're out there. Talk to me.

Zane heard nothing. He tried to see into the stands, but it was too dark.

Zane: Who are you?

Addict-Self: None of your business. I'm here to help you.

Zane: Come down here and talk to me face to face.

Addict-Self: I'm here and you're wasting time down there. Let's go work out at the club. We can watch women in those spandex suits you like.

Zane: What's your name? Tell me your name.

Addict-Self (*Looker*): You know who I am. I'm your friend. I'm Looker.

Zane: You're not my friend. You're hurting me. This time I want to see what you look like. I'm turning on the lights.

Looker: You're wasting time. Let's go look at the hotties in spandex.

Zane: Wait, I want to see you. C'mon down here into the light.

Looker: You don't need to see me. I've got your back. I know what you like. You like to see those women with their breasts and butts practically bursting out of their workout clothes.

Zane: I feel the pull to go to the workout club, but this time I'm going to turn on the lights.

Looker: You don't need to do that. Let's just go look at women so you can go home and jerk off. You know that's what you want.

Zane: I said come down here and talk to me face to face.

Looker: I can help you better if I'm in the dark.

Zane: But you're not helping me! I'm staying lonely. I want more. I want something real.

Looker: Something real? No, you don't want that. You want to look at those babes in their spandex and imagine them doing whatever you want them to do.

Zane: I'm turning on the lights now. I don't want you running my life from the dark anymore.

Next, Zane "turned on the lights" in his amphitheater—in this instance, the gymnasium—and he saw that this "Looker" was actually a twelve-year-old boy who liked to watch the girls when they were in gym class. They might have been in a class at the other end of the gym than his class, or he might have wandered into the gymnasium, or he might have seen them running outside on the soccer field.

In further dialogues with Looker, Zane remembered how, when he was nine, he stood in the darkness of his room and looked into his neighbor's window. Standing there, he watched an eighteen-year-old girl get ready for bed. It was this boy, Looker, who was trying to recapture the excitement Zane had felt as the boy. Once the light was turned on and Zane could see who the looker was and talk with that aspect of himself, that aspect lost some of its power over Zane's life and his sexual behavior.

For Zane, this dialogue with Looker continued, on and off, for weeks. This technique is a practice—it's not magic. Of course, the first time you try this, your addict might not want to talk and won't want you to turn the lights on. For the sake of your sanity, for the sake of the quality of your life, turn your lights on. Say something to get the conversation going. You could talk about starting your recovery. You could talk about how you know the addict-self is there. The point is to say something.

You might have to try talking to your addict subpersonality five or even many more times. Eventually it will become clear to you that this subpersonality isn't you. It represents your story. It's your history talking. Maybe your parents were mean to you. Maybe you went to your room and made up a porn story or you stole porn. Maybe your parents were drunk, and you found "company" in pornography or on the Internet.

Your addict-self up in the amphitheater is not your friend. It's that part of you that has split off and is afraid to talk to real women. Because of this fear, this part will continue to encourage you to pursue the false relationships of porn, prostitutes, phone sex, and so on.

I realize it's not easy to change your behavior or your mind. What if you find yourself in a porn shop, but you feel conflicted? What if you're at home, staring at porn on the computer screen? And in these moments, what if you had a dialogue with your addict-self? What if you play the part of being your own therapist and stir things up? Here's an example of what I stirred up with a client named Marv.

■ Marv Breaks with His Porn Addict

In his late thirties, Marv came to counseling to deal with his sex addiction so it would be more manageable. However, he still liked to go to porn shops. (Although this happened some years ago, before porn on the Internet became so big, you can experience something similar while sitting at your computer.)

I told Marv I'd meet him near his favorite porn shop and we would go in together. Marv knew I wanted his experience of porn shops to change, and he was not happy about it. His porn-addict voice was still very strong, and it was upset.

Despite having dialogued with it in his amphitheater, Marv was having difficulty making a break with his porn addict, and I wanted to be there, in the porn shop with him, to see if I could shift the balance so that my voice might become the voice Marv remembered the next time he wanted to visit a porn shop.

When I make an intervention, it's about changing the client's mind so that every time there's a possibility of engaging with porn, a prostitute, or other sexually compulsive behavior, he remembers the difficult experience he had with me in that situation. This gives him pause, even for a millisecond, which is a way for him to think about stopping. This gives him the opportunity to stop before his addictive energies start flowing.

When Marv and I walked into the porn shop, a big, muscular guy covered with tattoos was standing behind the counter. I looked at him and said loudly, "Hey, how you doing?" I kept trying to engage him in conversation, which is not something you're supposed to do in a porn shop. You're supposed to look down, except for furtive glances to see which aisle you want for the porn you like the most.

Tattoo Guy was not thrilled about me starting a conversation and, in a loud whisper, demanded to know what the fuck I wanted. I replied that Marv and I were just here looking, and I turned to Marv and loudly asked what it was in particular that he liked. Out of the side of his mouth, Marv mumbled, "Bondage." I then loudly repeated that we were looking for bondage.

Tattoo Guy was stressed. He was not usually asked for directions, but he pointed to aisle 3. As Marv and I walked to that aisle, I was still talking loudly. We started to get glances from other guys in the shop. Again, I was trying to provoke Marv to think differently, to have a different and *more realistic story about who goes to porn shops and the experience of being in such a shop.*

We got to the bondage aisle and I flipped open a magazine. I stopped at a photo of an anonymous woman tied to a bed. She was on her knees with her rear-end pointed at the camera. I very loudly said, "Wow, it looks like this woman sure has some bad hemorrhoids!"

Suddenly, two or three guys quickly walked out of the porn shop. It was difficult for them to stand being a part of that much reality. For the next few minutes, Marv and I continued looking at photos in the bondage magazines. Then, in a low, insistent voice, Marv said, "Okay, I get it. I don't want to be here." What Marv "got" was that porn is not real. It's fantasy. It's not even real sex. The addictive spell Marv had been under no longer had the same power over him. He had taken a big step in breaking free.

Confronting Your Addict in the Amphitheater

What I did with Marv is something that you can do with the addict subpersonality you meet in your amphitheater. You can continue the dialogue wherever you are. If you're at your computer looking at porn, at a strip club, or with a prostitute, you can even imagine me being there with you for a dose of reality. You can imagine me saying to you, "This woman is acting like she likes you, but how would she act if you weren't paying her?"

By dialoging with your addict in your amphitheater, you can change the dynamic so that the addict is no longer in control. In fact, the whole idea of imagining the amphitheater allows you to eventually run the show, instead of the stories you tell yourself being in charge. Every single thing you do as an addict—and much of the rest of the time—is the result of having thought about, read about, or done it before. It's based on stories. And you—the essence of you, or your essential self—have no need for any story. (We'll explore the idea of your essential self more in chapter 5.) Your essence is very wise. It keeps you out of trouble. It does the right thing instead of following a story that would lend itself better to a soap opera.

We're looking for a story of you that's an epic and not a soap opera. Your life may be wonderful in many areas, but it's only as strong as the weakest subpersonality. You're only as healthy as this subpersonality.

As I often remind my clients, you will experience resistance and sabotage. Some part of you will be reading this book and say, "I don't believe this. This guy's just an addictions counselor. Everyone is doing porn." But ask yourself these questions right now: Am I suffering? And why did I pick up this book?

You have to be relentless, more relentless than the Looker, the Drinker, the Porn Guy. You have to isolate a subpersonality, isolate the worst thing that's happening to you, and talk to it. If you isolate the worst thing that's happening to you, that will lead you to your negative subpersonality. If you actually do something about it, then you can change your mind—and this is the whole idea. The way to change your mind is to have more good things than bad things on your mind and in your mind so that you're a happier person with more calm in your life.

Confronting your subpersonalities is a way to reduce the pain and suffering in your life. If you're suffering, then it's very likely that you have one or more negative subpersonalities that cause you to do, think, and feel negative things. When that happens, you go into regression and you search your mental computer for something that will make you feel better. Are you doing that now? If so, how long do you want to continue to do that? The real question is: How good can you stand it? How much peace, joy, and serenity can you take? We'll look at this question more thoroughly in chapter 14.

Your amphitheater is always happening. Do you want to make use of it? Read the exercise below and just do it. Remember, it may not be easy, and it might not work well the first time you do it, but this exercise has worked again and again for people with sexually compulsive behavior just like you.

EXERCISE: Turn On the Lights and Face Your Addict

This exercise takes about fifteen minutes. Imagine yourself in your personal amphitheater with the lights on. You're looking at an offending negative subpersonality. What would you say to it? What questions would you ask?

Your first step is to give your addict a nickname. For example, my name is George and my addict's nickname is Porgie, as in Georgie Porgie. I've had clients give their addicts the nicknames the clients had as children, such as Danny for Daniel. Others name their addicts Hotshot, Loser, Mr. Jerkoff, and so on.

Talk to this addict subpersonality as if it were a real person. For example, ask, "Who are you? Why do you want me to act this particular way?" By doing this, you're tricking your mind so that you are in charge, rather than the story your mind tells you running the show. You begin to separate your thinking and your story from who you really are. Try to spend at least ten minutes a day on this exercise.

As you go through the next day, go to your amphitheater whenever your addict shows up, even if you spend only a few moments there. Your addict is an aspect of you, it's a complex, a subpersonality. Talk to it. Try to write down your dialogue while you're imagining it, or do that later if you have to. Writing down the dialogue will give the experience a stronger impact. If you just think about it, it won't work as well because it won't seem as important to your mind.

Remember, the mind doesn't like to change, and you need to use whatever leverage you can. If you keep going to the amphitheater and conducting dialogues with your addict, your thoughts will have less power over you and you will begin to feel more in charge. And, as you feel more empowered, you'll be able to act in ways that are contrary to what your addict wants. The next chapter will describe how Larry learned to say no to his addict subpersonality, and I'll explain how you can take additional steps to break free of negative thoughts.

CHAPTER 3

You Are Not Your Mind

Your life can be seen as a soap opera written and directed by your mind. And in every soap opera, there's always a character that is going to screw up. One of the voices that calls out to you from your personal amphitheater is the Screwup. What this book offers you is the ability to rewrite your story. You can change that character so that it no longer causes divorces, loss of jobs, or other problems. You can discover that it's your mind that has made up the story you believe about yourself. And you are not your mind.

Your Mind Is Like a Library

You could think of your mind as a giant library of information composed of memories, feelings, and projections. Its thoughts are based on what's already happened and on projections of what you think might happen in the future. Everything that ever happened to you is recorded in this archive. Any time your senses focus on something in your environment, your unconscious mind processes it to make sure it's safe or edible, or to objectify it, or whatever the case may be—all based on your historical recollections. "Memory is often thought of as the change within an individual, brought on by learning, that can influence the individual's future behavior" (Gray 2006, 303).

When I was stuck in my mind, every piece of pizza I ate was based on my early experiences of eating at Cutters Bar & Grill in Morristown, New Jersey. Every time I ate a pizza, I unconsciously compared it to the pizza at Cutters, which may or may not have been great. But it was so exciting to eat pizza as a boy with my family that my criteria in my adult life were based on eating pizza at Cutters in 1954. That childhood experience became what is called my *euphoric recall* for eating pizza. My practice is now to try to do everything as if it were happening for the first time. It's not always easy. Guess what? Mind does not want to change, even for the better.

Cutting Through Euphoric Recall

Most of us also have euphoric recall for sexual experiences. Author and psychotherapist Alexandra Katehakis wrote that "addicts may engage in the euphoria that comes with recalling past sexual experiences, labeled 'euphoric recall.' They may also fantasize about some future sexual exploit. What's the outcome of these activities? The sexual experience becomes an avoidance of connection with their partner and their own feelings in the present" (Katehakis, 2010, 33).

There is so much for each of us to see freshly in the present, without comparing. It's really important to be in the moment and to do everything that we do, including sexual activity, as if it's the first time. Avoid remembering how great the sex was when you first masturbated or when you saw your first porn. Avoid thinking of what it was like to be in the backseat of the car with your first girlfriend. Euphoric recall will take you away from your current experience. In addition, for many, euphoric recall is the act of "remembering only the pleasures of an experience and not the adverse consequences" (Rawson and Urban 2000, 73). That's why it's important to experience what's happening now versus what's in your euphoric memory, which may be distorted.

Euphoric recall is a function of your mind and your memory. This is why you should remember that you are not your mind. You are not your memories. You can live a more fulfilling life in the moment. As Eckhart Tolle wrote, "Your mind is an instrument, a tool. It is there to be used for a specific task, and when the task is completed, you lay it down. As it is, I would say about 80 to 90 percent of most people's thinking is not only repetitive and useless, but because of its dysfunctional and often negative nature, much of it is also harmful. Observe your mind and you will find this to be true" (Tolle 1999, 14).

■ Larry Takes a Stand with His Porn Addict

Larry is a young man involved in the music business in Nashville. Larry's father was a very successful attorney, and Larry's brothers and sisters all decided early on to also become attorneys. Unlike them, Larry was shy and was not drawn to the law. Larry felt left out. He wasn't like his siblings, and he came to believe that he wasn't good enough. This false belief compounded his social awkwardness. Masturbation became a coping mechanism and a way for him to avoid social contact.

Larry loved country music. He attended a vocational training college and moved to Nashville to pursue his dream of working in the music business. Despite not knowing anyone *in Nashville, with his education and his passion for the music, Larry was hired at a low-level position. But outside of work, Larry was lonely.*

As he had done earlier in his life, Larry went to strip clubs and watched porn. Because he was shy, rather than trying to date a real woman, it seemed so much easier to indulge himself with masturbation. Larry would spend hours and hours on porn sites, searching for the perfect woman with perfect breasts in the perfect sexual situation. When his sexually compulsive behavior began to greatly interfere with his concentration on the job, Larry contacted me. We worked together for months. Finally, Larry was able to make a different choice.

One night at a bar after listening to a band that his boss was considering signing to a recording contract, Larry walked back to his car. It was late and, as usual, he was about to drive home alone. Across the street from his car he saw the lights of a porn shop. It was, of course, open until midnight. Larry walked over to the porn shop and debated with himself about going inside. Standing in front of the shop, Larry used his smartphone to text me the dialog he was having with his addict, whom he called "Porn Guy."

Larry: I know what's happening. I can feel the pull.

Porn Guy: Then what are you waiting for? Let's go!

Larry: I know you have a tremendous desire to go into this porn shop and get momentary gratification.

Porn Guy: That's right! Let's go!

Larry: I'm going to stand here for a few minutes and just experience your pull, Porn Guy.

Porn Guy: What're you talking about?! C'mon! You've never stopped before! Don't stop now!

Larry: In experiencing the pull, I can get beyond it. I can continue to say it's not a good idea. I'm not going to walk away. I'm going to fully experience the desire to do this, but I'm not going to do it.

Porn Guy: Oh, for fuck's sake! Stop being such a wuss! Just go on in!

Larry: No. I'm choosing to move forward with my life. I'm taking a stand!

Then Larry walked back to his car and drove home.

Larry later told me that he knew that the way to move forward was to stand still for a minute and let his negative subpersonality, Porn Guy, try to persuade him. But Larry was able to take a stand with his addict.

That was a turning point for Larry. In taking a stand against his addict, Larry transcended his negative subpersonality, which was pounding on him to concede and go in to buy porn.

You Can Say No to Your Addict

Larry was able to take a stand because he had done enough work on his sexually compulsive behavior that it was no longer completely automatic. He had reached a point where he could make a choice. It wasn't easy, but he did it—just as you can. As long as you don't give up and you keep moving forward, you will have the opportunity to say no to your addict, just as Larry did.

Some of my clients have described this experience as a death. Not a death of themselves, but a death of the old story in their mind that kept them doing the same thing over and over again. Even if it's a death, it's also a "dying" into life, a dying into a better story and taking more positive steps. Once you realize that you are not your mind, you are not your story, you can begin to break from your story. Then you'll finally have the possibility of relating intimately to a real person.

In Larry's case, he took some steps to socialize with others that would not put too much pressure on him. For example, he started going on bicycle rides with groups of people. On one such ride, a woman he had noticed before rode her bike beside him and they started talking. Her name was Lisa. Talking led to dating. Larry decided to let nature take its course rather than trying to persuade her to have sex immediately.

As problems came up, they discussed their issues. They dated for several weeks before they had sex. Larry was very clear that sex was not the most important part of their relationship. He was interested in being with Lisa, sharing ideas, and understanding women in general and Lisa in particular. For men who have mostly experienced the fantasy world of strip clubs and pornography, when they get to know these incredible people called women, it's fascinating. They wonder: What's going on with her? What's her story? And how does that relate to me?

Larry and Lisa became a couple. The possibility of a real relationship began when Larry understood that he was not his mind. He was not his thoughts. He was not Porn Guy, who wanted only to watch porn. He had taken a stand.

Your Mind Is Not Who You Are

About ten years after I completed my studies in graduate school, I had the good fortune to experience the teachings of several spiritual teachers, especially Eckhart Tolle. Up until that time I had believed that I was "only" this body, a seething mass of mostly semicontrolled feelings, emotions, and actions. Through my studies in graduate school, I was able to understand and change my emotional makeup. But when I read the book *The Power of Now*, I experienced myself in a new way, a way that I could not have logically anticipated. I began to understand "identification with [my] mind, which causes thought to become compulsive. Not to be able to stop thinking is a dreadful affliction, but we don't realize this because almost everybody is suffering from it, so it is considered normal" (Tolle 1999, 5).

I would never have thought that I was not my mind. As a "regular guy," I wondered what that meant. I suddenly realized that if I was not my mind, then I was also not my thoughts—the thoughts that made up the story that I told myself about myself and my compulsions. During my childhood, I had listened to what my parents and teachers had to say to me and to teach me. I also observed their actions toward others and me. From those teachings and observations, I developed a story—the story of George. But I didn't even know I had this story because I thought I *was* the story, rather than being separate from it. I didn't think about it as bad or good, but just kept living my life according to this script.

Well, this would have been "all good" if it had been a good story, but my early years were filled with abuse, both physical and emotional. Although my parents did the best they could, they were operating from their own sad and difficult stories. Most of my story was based on my home situation and how my parents related to me and to each other. I grew up feeling "less than," ashamed, afraid, angry, and judgmental, which was similar to how my parents felt about themselves. Feeling that way about myself was my norm. I didn't understand that it was negative for me to feel this way, but I did understand that I needed to do something to feel better. To compensate for what I thought of as my character defects, I developed coping strategies. These coping behaviors were meant to help me feel better, if even for a moment. My coping strategy involved the objectification of women. As a boy, it was fun and pleasurable to look at naked and half-naked women in catalogues and magazines, such as *National Geographic*.

My father talked "dirty" and read pornographic magazines. My mother exhibited inappropriate nudity and suggestive sexual talk toward me in a way that would be called emotionally incestuous. "Emotionally incestuous parents turn to their children to satisfy needs that should be satisfied by other adults—namely intimacy, companionship, romantic stimulation, advice, problem solving, ego fulfillment, and/or emotional release" (Engel 2010, 45).

My situation with my parents was too much for my young mind to handle. I split off emotionally and began smoking cigarettes, drinking alcohol, and obsessing about sexual matters that I wasn't old enough to truly understand. I was living this story at the direction of my young mind, which was still largely under the influence of my parents.

Years later, when I began to understand that I wasn't my mind (and therefore not my story), I started to become free. That is what you can do, too. Now, I can actually be in the moment, at least a great deal of the time, and not live and act in reaction to my history. I can watch my mind as it makes decisions and plans what to do next. I can then, usually, intercept and alter my thinking if it's heading in a nonproductive, compulsive direction.

■ *Joey Separates Himself from His Mind*

Here is another example of a dialogue in which a man I'll call Joey talks with his addict subpersonality. Joey has been having these dialogues for long enough to begin to experience that he is not his mind. Joey calls his subpersonality "Mind."

Joey: You have been active on the negative side this past weekend.

Mind: That's my job. We have to think, especially about sex.

Joey: Waking up in the morning, and at other times, I can hear all the negative, self-hating voices really jump out at me.

Mind: Yes! Yes! Have to think, have to think!

Joey: We don't have to think all the time. We can just be silent inside.

Mind: No, no. We can't stop. We need to be thinking about things, imagining, planning. We can't stop.

Joey: We can stop. Or we can, at least, pause. It isn't that hard.

Mind: Run, run. There is too much to think about.

Joey: We can settle this by watching ourselves think. I am also curious why you sometimes jump into this fierce self-hatred. What's going on there?

Mind: Have to think about something. And it's easy to think about things you've screwed up—either yesterday, or ten years ago, or twenty years ago. Those are easy, and we can think about those.

Joey: Okay, yes, screwups do seem to bubble to the surface easier than other things. But you can help me by flagging this and reminding me to watch.

Mind: Maybe. Gotta run. Gotta think.

Joey: Just try. Try to think about watching. Okay?

Mind: Okay.

By "watching," Joey means that he wants to notice his thoughts, watch them, and experience himself as separate from the thoughts of his mind. It's the mind that perpetuates your story.

EXERCISE: Notice That You Are More Than Your Thoughts

This exercise could take only a minute, but you're welcome to take longer. The important thing is to be consciously aware that you are not your mind. Go to a quiet, private place with low light and as little sound as possible. Sit down for a few minutes. Stop everything. Stop your mind. Just be aware that you exist. Even if you can manage to stop your mind for only two seconds, do it. Just be aware of your existence, not your story. Not any story. You just *are*.

Start with just a second or two. Now, I'm not trying to turn you into a meditating monk. But you need to experience the tremendous difference between who *you* are and the *story* of you. Once you realize that you are not your story, you can begin to take your stories apart. You may have an eating addiction that is not you. You may be in a job that you don't like. But you are not your job.

Stop and look to see what subpersonality is speaking and try to find out what's going on. If sexual images and memories come up, try naming your subpersonality and dialoguing with it. Be more objective with yourself and ask your subpersonality what's going on. Ask yourself, "Where and when did this start, and what do I have to do to change?"

I encourage you to do this every day for one month while reading this book.

One of my key phrases with my counseling clients is "Take my job." What I do as a counselor is help a client bring his false stories and myths into the light so he no longer automatically assumes that his thoughts are always true. Similarly, by dialoguing with your subpersonalities and noticing your thoughts, you can take my job as a counselor and uncover your own false stories and myths. This book will provide you with the tools to *demystify*— clearly see the associations you have with—your false stories and to break free of your sexually compulsive behavior.

If you find yourself sitting there saying, "I don't have a story," you're in denial. Everybody has a story. If you feel the need to deny your story, is it because you want a better story? Even when you get a better story, it's important not to keep that one, either— because you'll be missing something even better. Continue to watch your mind and, when necessary, take a stand against it.

In the next chapter, we'll do some rudimentary detective work to search out clues to uncovering your unique story. For now, begin to work on taking a stand with your mind so that you can stop the incessant overthinking that can lead to self-destructive behavior. Be with yourself and observe that you are not your mind. You are not your thoughts. Begin to experience that you are something more than what your mind says.

CHAPTER 4

C.S.I.—Clues to Your Unique Story

Just as in the *C.S.I.* TV shows, think of this chapter as an adventure in which you discover clues about yourself and uncover the mystery of your story. What I mean by "your story" will become increasingly clear as you read further. Your compulsive behavior is based on your story. If you want to learn how you can live your life differently, you need to step back and change how you look at things. That's what this chapter is about: seeing your story and stepping outside of it. To paraphrase a line from Albert Einstein: in order to solve a problem, you can't use the same thinking that got you into the problem.

Your Addict's Story: It's Fiction, Not Fact

By unraveling your history, you can uncover your story to take the first step toward understanding that you are not your story. To do this, you need to be something of a detective. You need to uncover the facts in order to get to the truth. In this case, it's the truth of who you are. By uncovering your story, you will disempower your story and empower yourself to live without giving in to your compulsions. It's not easy, but you can do it.

■ *Ryan Connects His History with His Sex Addiction*

Ryan was a professional baseball player who had grown up with a mother who didn't pay much attention to him and a father who was a playboy. Ryan's father was a salesman who pretended to have much more money than he actually had. Consequently, his family always lived beyond its means. When Ryan was a boy, his family's pretentions all felt phony. In taking his history, Ryan saw a connection between growing up with the lack of intimacy between his parents and his current sexually compulsive behavior.

Because no intimacy between family members had ever been modeled for Ryan, he had never learned how to be intimate with others. Ryan had learned only to pretend, just as he had seen his father do. (When we're young, we are like little sponges—absorbing the behaviors modeled by our parents.) Even though Ryan had realized as a boy that his home life felt inauthentic, he didn't know another way to live. Consequently, as an adult he was still pretending and didn't know how to truly connect with a woman.

Ryan had sought some sort of stability and had married a stripper. But, because the marriage had been built on pretense and appearances rather than on intimacy, after they had children, Ryan's incredibly sexy wife became "just" a busy, caring mother who made their kids' lunches with curlers in her hair and no makeup. His ideas about what his wife "should" look like were being shattered. So, like his father before him, Ryan felt the urge to look elsewhere.

By uncovering his history, Ryan saw how the pretense and lack of intimacy in his family of origin had left an emotional scar that Ryan coped with through his sexually compulsive behavior. This inner scar was the key component of Ryan's story—a story that needed to be remade from the inside out. By pretending the family was better off than they were, Ryan's father had encouraged a fantasy life as opposed to living in the truth of real intimacy.

You may think your childhood or teenage years are far in the past and have nothing to do with you now. That's fiction. The truth is that if you, as little Ryan or Bobby or Carla or Suzie, saw your mommy and daddy as friends and lovers who held hands and kissed, you grew up with a more positive version of male-female relationships. If Daddy was focused on affairs, or he staggered into the house angry and drunk, dragged Mommy into the bedroom, and slammed the door, you grew up with a different model of male-female relationships. There are many gradations in between. Everyone reading this book has a unique history and story. Understanding your own history—and the story you made from it—gives you the power to discover which past events and associations you are still allowing to unconsciously control you through your compulsive behavior.

■ *Keith and the Cheerleader*

Keith was a successful businessman whose marriage was failing. While he was growing up, Keith's mother and father didn't have much interest in him and often left him in the care of a babysitter. By the time he was twelve, Keith was a handsome boy. One day a new babysitter, an attractive sixteen-year-old blonde cheerleader, was watching him. (We don't intend any sexist reference by referring to a cheerleader, and it's a fact that many men in this country have an obsession with cheerleaders.) She started being playful with Keith, which led to touching him and more.

When Keith had sex with the cheerleader during this formative and vulnerable time in his life, she became his blueprint for relationships with women. Over the course of a year, Keith's experiences with her shaped his ideas about what intimacy and love were "supposed" to be. In other words, Keith's personal history determined his story of how love and intimacy should look in his life.

Be a Crime-Scene Investigator for Your Unique History

Maybe you read about Keith and thought, "I'd like to have that cheerleader in *my* history." However, if a similar relationship was a part of your experience, a history of true intimacy might be missing from your life. Like Keith, you could be stuck in a steaming heap of compulsive behavior that prevents you from having a satisfying marriage, a healthy focus on your work, and as much success in life as you could have.

By becoming a detective and unraveling your history, you can uncover your story, which is the first step to understanding that you are *not* your story. This comprehension is vital, because stories created in and by your childhood are no longer relevant. Operating according to these stories is like running on software that was installed when you were a child. It's obsolete. Reviewing your history (called "taking a history" by therapists) will give you the information you need to find the old software and update it. So far, I've given you a simplified overview of what an examination of your history can uncover. Later in this chapter you'll see a sampling of the specific questions that I ask clients to answer in this exploration. The point is for you to act like a C.S.I. does to uncover the facts in order to get the truth—the truth of who you actually are.

We're being detectives now. You and I, together, are looking for clues to the origins of your compulsive behavior. As with any detective story, the detecting work can be interesting and even fun. I'll provide the search parameters and you'll do the legwork. You might also think of your quest to uncover your history as a Google search for the origins of your compulsive suffering.

Answer the questions or, if you don't have immediate answers, reflect on the them and notice your thoughts now and over time. Write notes on paper for your answers, or type on your computer, or just think about the answers. I'll add some hints to help you see what you need to see, so you'll gain clues for understanding why you act the way you do. Remember, you're looking for information, not ammunition. This self-inquiry is meant to help you *help* yourself, not to criticize yourself or others. Bear in mind, your parents did the best they could. Taking your history is not a way of blaming.

Also, your addict is not your enemy, but a worthy adversary. Your addict personality actually believes it's helping you. This is a trick of the mind—a false story. Uncovering your history uncovers the truth. Step back and look, as if you are seeing someone else—a witness to your own life, your unique addict. That way you can become an understanding, empathetic advocate for yourself and your addict. Now let's get started.

Taking Your History

Writing down your behavior, or even thinking about it and how long you have been doing it, may be difficult. But writing and thinking about your behavior is an essential step in changing it. When a person with sexually compulsive behavior is in counseling with me, it's my job to ask questions in order to get to the truth. By asking yourself the questions, you get to be the detective. As if you were Sherlock Holmes working to solve a case, you need to pay close attention to the answers to the questions—the clues. They are pieces of the puzzle of why you think and behave the way you do, and why you've created the story you're living by now. Now take out your journal or notepad, or sit down at your computer, and answer the following questions as best you can.

How Did Your Sexually Compulsive Behavior Start?

Let's begin by looking at some questions to ask yourself about your past. These may help you to discover when your compulsive sexual behavior began, and that will help you to understand how and why you've constructed the story you tell yourself about your sexual addiction.

As a child, maybe you were lonely and you found your father's porn. Or maybe in junior high you were rejected by a girl you'd thought about for years, and then decided it was easier to fantasize about women than risk rejection again. If you don't know when your sexually compulsive behavior began, just try to see the events of your life from a new, more informed, "C.S.I." vantage point.

I want to stress that, if you write down your answers to all of these questions, you may find that your understanding of your own story will deepen and you may begin to view yourself with more compassion. Take as much time as you need to answer these questions. Even if you need several days to dig up the details, keep trying. It will be worth it. Even Sherlock Holmes had to search for clues.

■ How old are you now, and how long have you been doing the same or different sexually compulsive behaviors?

■ When you were a child, did you play doctor? Did your compulsive behavior start with the girl next door? Or the boy next door?

■ How did you learn about sex? That is, how was sex introduced to you? Did you have "the talk" (about sex) with your parents or with another authority figure?

■ Did the other kids talk about sex? What did they say to you? Did it frighten or arouse you?

■ Was there anything good about how you learned about sex?

■ Did you masturbate when you were young? How young were you?

■ Did anything change after you'd had sex? Did it affect your experience of touching yourself? Of orgasm? What changed in how you felt about yourself before and after you had sex?

■ Were you lonely as an adolescent? Hurt by girls?

■ Do you feel that you have to continue to use prostitutes, masturbation, or pornography to achieve sexual satisfaction? On the porn sites, in strip clubs, and in massage parlors, women pretend to want you. Their job is to act a part and take your money. What do the women at a strip club do when a customer runs out of twenties? You know the answer to that.

When you were young, maybe your feelings were hurt over and over because of rejections from your parents or potential girlfriends. You may have needed some other way to find satisfaction. You may have thought you needed to fantasize about a girl really wanting you. And that may be the story that you continue to tell yourself today.

Does Your Occupation Have Anything to Do with Your Addiction?

A client once said to me, "I like my job because it goes quickly, and it's Friday before I know it." I said to myself, *Five days out of the week this guy is suffering so he can get to the weekend—when he thinks he can have fun.* That's not what I want for my clients or for the readers of this book.

- Do you smile and are you pleased to be there when you walk into your workplace? Or do you wish it were already 5 p.m.?

- Some people have sales jobs so they will have unstructured time out on the road to stop in to strip clubs and porn shops. What part has your addiction played in your choice of jobs?

One of your goals while reading and working with this book might be to learn how to convert the energy used by your sexual addiction into positive adult behavior, including the big question: what do you want to do with your life?

What Is Your Past and Present Relationship Status?

Thinking back over your past relationships may give you clues regarding your relationship patterns and behavior:

- When you were in high school, did you date? Were you a jock or a geek? Or were you so isolated that you didn't identify with any group?

- Were you terrified to talk to girls? Or were you sociable? Did you go to the prom, or were you reclusive?

- Can you imagine having the feelings you have when you're by yourself being replaced by intimacy with someone you share your whole life with?

Your answers to these questions all have something to do with how you perceive sex today. Everyone, including you, lives his or her life constantly reacting to his or her history.

Do You Have Nonaddictive Hobbies?

When I ask new clients about hobbies, they often look at me with astonishment. "What do you think I do? I go to strip clubs or online porn sites." A lot of sex addicts forget to have "regular" hobbies or to take part in any other activities but sex. Answer these questions:

- What do you read? Do you read for pleasure or only for information?

- Are you physically active? Do you exercise?

- What kind of movies do you like?

- If you don't have any nonsexual hobbies, can you think of some that might appeal to you?

If "Nope" was your answer to the last question, it could be that you can't think of any other enjoyable activities because your strongest answer has always been, "I do porn." Listen for another answer and look around you. There are lots of fun and interesting activities available. The real F word is "fun."

What Is the Financial Impact of Your Compulsive Behavior?

By "financial impact," I don't mean just the money you spend on porn or other sexually compulsive behavior, although that can be considerable. Time spent on porn could be time spent making money. I've had clients who, over a period of years, wasted hundreds of thousands of dollars on their compulsive sexual addictions. Consider:

- How much time do you spend thinking about sex?

- How much time do you spend engaging in sexually compulsive behavior?

- How much money do you spend on sexually compulsive behavior?

- Does the time you spend thinking about or engaging in sexually compulsive behavior cut into the time you could be working productively and earning money or engaging in an enjoyable hobby or an intimate relationship?

How Does Your Family History Relate to Your Addiction?

Remember, and this is important, your parents did the best they could under the circumstances. Taking your history is about *you* understanding how what happened influenced your life and moving forward. Remember, you're seeking information, not ammunition. Ask yourself:

- Did your mother and father have an active social life?

- Were you invited to social gatherings? Was there drinking involved?

- Did your father have male friends? Was your mother upset with him because he wanted to go to baseball games or play cards with his friends?

- Did your mother have women friends?

- Did your family move a lot? If so, how did that impact you?

If, when you were growing up, you moved a lot, you probably had your feelings hurt when you were forced to leave friends behind. If you didn't develop the ability to have friendships when you were younger, it would be difficult for you to know how to be a good friend to your wife or partner. Nevertheless, the social skills required to maintain friendship and intimacy can be learned.

Were There Traumatic Events in Your History?

Traumatic events can impact your sexuality and lead to coping behaviors such as sexual addiction.

Consider:

- Was there ever sexual contact with anyone in your family? If so, were there any consequences?

- Did you have brothers or sisters? Was there abuse? If there was, was it emotional, physical, or sexual—or a combination?

- Was there violence? When? With whom? Did you get yelled at a lot? Were you hit or in any other way physically abused?

- Was there any sexual abuse from a parent or another family member?

- Were you angry or upset about treatment you received from your primary caregiver or parent, who was supposed to be a person you trusted more than anyone else in the world?

If someone hurt you or scared you when you were a child, even many years later you may have a tendency to isolate, which leads to unstructured time. If your parents proved untrustworthy, or you were beaten, yelled at, or sexually abused, it's likely you tended to isolate. Isolation leads to addiction. People like connection. If we are forced by circumstances (including trauma), we may isolate, make up stories, and have pretend girlfriends. This is because it feels safer and easier not to connect with a real person. Many people who had sex with a parent or sibling became sex addicts because of their shame. "Although shame is very often tied to sexual abuse, shame can result from any type of abuse" (Knauer 2002, 78).

Can you see how having been abused might have taught you to "compartmentalize" (nice guy on the outside—tortured inside) or might have split you into what appears to be two different parts—causing you to become isolated and to fear intimate relationships with others? Some of my clients report feeling almost as if they were two people.

How Was Alcohol Used in Your Family?

Although alcoholism is not the cause of sex addiction, studies have shown a strong correlation between sex addiction and substance abuse (Adams and Carnes 2002). I have also consistently seen a strong connection between sex addiction and alcohol use with clients in my counseling practice. Consider these questions about alcohol:

■ How did your parents behave when they drank?

■ How did that make you feel?

■ What did you do about it? Maybe you left the house. Or you might have hidden yourself from them. You might have found some porn to occupy you.

■ Do you drink too much now?

Does Your Social Networking Relate to Your Sex Addiction?

Humans are social animals, and when sociability is absent, we seek other ways to relate. If you felt isolated, you may have sought ways to connect, such as going to chat rooms.

When social networking is done online in sexual situations, many of the people you communicate with are sitting at their computers masturbating. Based on what I've been told by clients, more than half the time when you think you're talking to a woman online, having free "phone sex" in a chat room, it's actually a man on the other end of the line, and usually a man who is not gay. You may wonder why a man would do this. Some of my clients are so isolated that they cannot even try to be sexual on chat lines with women. So they pretend to be a woman and chat online with a man while they masturbate. When my clients hear about men imitating women online, it helps to break down their fantasy world. I've had clients tell me, "George, you've ruined it for me. Now every time I go to a chat room to talk sex with a woman, I wonder if I'm really talking to some screwed-up dude." So the next time you're on a chat line thinking you're talking to a sexy woman, remember that it's entirely possible that you're engaging with a man.

Do You Feel Guilty About Sex?

One huge component that fuels sex addiction is guilt. Many gay people grew up hearing from their families and the culture that their sexuality was bad or forbidden. Today, for many young people, sexual orientation has become a nonissue. But even among some heterosexual families, sex was considered bad or dirty. When I was a sex addict, I was looking to connect with someone who really wanted me. Guilt drove my addiction. This is true in general—guilt drives addiction. Ask:

- How was the topic of sexuality treated in your family?

- What role does guilt play in your life?

- Has your sexual orientation influenced your sexually compulsive behavior?

- I've had gay clients who've internalized society's homophobia. If you are gay, how long did you have to keep your sexuality a secret?

- Did you internalize homophobia?

- Did your parents tell you they loved you whether or not you were gay? Did you talk to them about it?

I have seen bisexuals who felt confused and guilty because they were not straight, and some felt even more guilt because they were not gay. Unraveling their history has helped some bisexual people to alleviate their guilt.

I have counseled supposedly straight male clients who are so hooked on orgasm that they'll go to "glory holes" at rest stops and public lavatories to get blow jobs from gay men three or four times a week.

Do You Have Abnormal or Scary Thoughts?

Your answers to the questions in this section could be warning signs that you need to talk to a professional and not just read this book. Ask yourself:

- Have you had any thoughts of harming yourself or others?

- Compared to the people you know at work or in your social circle, how abnormal is your thinking?

- Do you wish you were dead?

- Do you find yourself thinking that you would like to hurt yourself or someone else?

- Do you have other addictions or behaviors that are self-destructive?

- Are you overdoing drugs and alcohol to the point of blacking out?

- Are you overeating to the point where you are morbidly obese?

Consider Your History

You were shaped by your early experiences. Your sexually compulsive behavior isn't just about sex. It's about your self-esteem. It's about everything that ever happened to you, especially the negative experiences that sparked you to seek a coping strategy such as visiting prostitutes or using the Internet for porn.

You need to learn how to convert the energy from your negative experiences into positive adult behavior, thought, and action. Can you think about what else you might like to do besides your compulsive behavior?

It's not easy to stop. You may have a deep, gnawing, harsh sensation that says you can't stop. Your addict subpersonality might say: "You must do this. You must go to Internet porn sites. You can't change." However, if you've been practicing the amphitheater-dialogue technique from chapter 2, you may have begun to shift away from the power of your compulsion.

I changed, and I've worked with hundreds of clients who have also changed their sexually compulsive behavior. You can too. Along the way, you may need to use certain techniques to help you through the transition and others to keep you focused once you've changed your behavior. The following exercise is a technique that will help you to make the transition.

EXERCISE: Find Your Beard Test

This is an exercise that you can do in a few seconds any time it's necessary. Run your open palm across your cheek, moving from your neck up toward your eyes (opposite the way your facial hair grows). If it makes a noise, you're a man. I call this the Beard Test. It's something I do when I occasionally catch myself objectifying women or I notice myself feeling young or immature. It's a simple test you can do anywhere and at any time to remind you that you are an adult. Try the Beard Test or find your own version. It works if you *work* it.

You don't have to live in reaction to your history. There are no pimples on your face anymore. You have a beard now, and when rubbed, it makes a noise. There are times when I'm in a restaurant and my wife will ask, "Where is she?" "What?" I might respond, innocently. Then my wife will say she saw me doing the Beard Test, and we may look around to see the woman whom my addict may have unconsciously objectified. I also do the Beard Test when I spend more than three seconds looking at a woman. I call this "The Three-Second Rule." Sometimes I don't even know I'm doing the Beard Test. It has become a positive, unconscious behavior that I do to correct my old addictive story line.

It would be helpful for you to use the Beard Test or to create your own reminder ritual. A *reminder ritual* is a small behavior to prompt yourself to remember that you are an adult and that you no longer need to engage in behaviors that will only bring you suffering. While you are unraveling the history of your compulsive behavior, and while you're reading and working with this book and learning that you are not your mind or your addict, you may need to find or create new ways to deal with your sexually compulsive behavior. The Beard Test is one method that can help you stay on the path to freedom.

In the next chapter we'll explore another step that can enable you to stop thinking of yourself as an addict and to see yourself as so much more.

CHAPTER 5

What's Always True:
Knowing Your Essential Self

When you have a compulsive desire to act out sexually, understanding what's always true can bring you back to yourself so that you are in control. This chapter explains how "what's always true" is a technique to help you stay in the moment so that you don't react in a negative way.

An Addiction to Your Mind

Your real addiction is to your mind. If your mind does not change, it will operate in the same way, day after day, providing you with a life sentence of sexually compulsive behavior. In chapters 2 and 3 you learned that you are not your mind and that there is a lot going on in that amphitheater between your ears. But what to do about it? In my graduate training, I studied a modality called "psychosynthesis." According to psychologist Roberto Assagioli, *psychosynthesis* is "that form of synthesis that expresses the will of the Higher Self" (Assagioli 1965, 61). In Assagioli's view, individuals greatly benefit by becoming familiar with their subpersonalities. One method for accomplishing this is through the dialogue work I described in chapter 2, where you turned on the lights in your amphitheater.

Once you see the different subpersonalities in your amphitheater and understand that you're really not your story, what you can do is "talk" to your subpersonalities. You can actually carry on a conversation with one or more subpersonalities, and by doing so you can start the process of changing your mind.

You Are Separate from Your Subpersonalities

Earlier in the book you read examples of dialogues in which a person talked to his addictive subpersonality called Porn Guy and another man talked to his Looker subpersonality. You may have started a dialogue with your own Prostitute Pete, Stripper-Club Guy, or Chat-Room Charlie. Now imagine yourself in your amphitheater with the lights on. You're looking at the offending negative subpersonality or subpersonalities. By imagining seeing them as separate from you, you can begin to get a sense that you are more than these subpersonalities and, furthermore, that you are in charge.

To reiterate, your subpersonalities are a part of your mind, and mind does not like to change. Mind will do anything it can to distract you. That is one reason I encourage you not just to imagine your dialogues with your subpersonalities, but also to write them down. Writing causes you to focus and encourages your mind to remember. In that way, it helps you to change.

This chapter will take the idea that you are not your mind, from chapter 3, a step further, helping you to experience the truth that you are bigger than your story. You have what many, including Roberto Assagioli, call a "higher self," though I prefer the terms "essential self" and "essence." All of these terms refer to what is always true about you.

There is nothing religious about having an essence. It is not New Age woo-woo. It's what you were born with. It's the essential nature of you. Your mind may balk at considering that there is something more to you than your thoughts. That is your mind attempting to stay in charge. If you go beyond your mind to your essential self, you can experience that you are the one who is truly in charge.

What Is Always True Is That You Are in Charge

Your subpersonalities are playing out your story. They have an investment in wanting you to continue your story, whether that story is that you need to visit prostitutes or chat rooms for sex or that you need porn because all women will reject or hurt you. This is the tail wagging the dog. What you should be learning is how to wag the tail instead of it wagging you.

Once you experience that you are not your story, you can feel yourself being in charge of your life. You can be in your essence. You do not have to listen to your addict self. It is not who you are. You are the one who is always in charge.

If a subpersonality tells you that you will be a better person if you have sex with a prostitute, that is not true. If a subpersonality says that you have to have an orgasm in the next ten minutes or you will nosedive into depression, that is not true. If a subpersonality tells you that the woman on the chat line wants you to keep talking at a fee just because she really likes you as a person, that is not true. But that part of you that is the essence of you is always true. Once you get in touch with it, you can count on it. It's there for you. It has your best interests at heart.

Here is an example of one of my clients, Brian, having a conversation with the part of himself that is always true—his essence.

Brian: You there? I need you.

Essence: I'm here. Always here.

Brian: I forget.

Essence: Try not to. I can help. I know you. I am you. I am you at your best. I am who you really are.

Brian: I'm still objectifying.

Essence: I see that. It hurts you. That's not who we really are. Remember, you want intimacy with one woman. Remember?

Brian: I do now. But sometimes I forget.

Essence: Remember, your desire for intimacy is what's always true. Your conditioning said, "Get a lot of pussy. She's hot. I'd like to get in her pants." That's not you, Brian. You want to love and be loved...deeply. You learned that stuff, but now you're awake to me...your essence...what's always true. Do you hear me?

Brian: Yes. It feels *so* good to know that you are actually within me. That I am actually you. That I know the truth. Stay here. Will you?

Essence: I'm always here. Always will be. You just didn't know that. No one told you. No one knew.

Brian: Whew! So good. Sooo good. I wish I'd known about you years ago.

Essence: Brian, stop worrying about that. You know now. Be here now.

Conscious Awareness Is Always True

Who you think you are is this bundle of experiences based on your sensory perceptions in any given moment. Your mind is constantly spinning stories, and these stories stop you from being in the present—because they're not actually true. What *is* always true is your conscious awareness. It's being aware that you're conscious and present, without being stimulated by a pizza or a beer or a woman. What's always true is pure conscious awareness—just being.

You've been trained to do multitasking, to do as many things as you can do. So, you're often more of a "human doing" rather than a "human being." But constantly doing removes you from yourself, because you're not just *being*. The question I have for you is this: Can you just be for a second? For ten seconds? Just ask yourself that question, without worrying about what the answer is. You're not trying to find the answer to the question, "What's always true?" What's always true is your essence.

If you ask yourself what's always true when you're standing in line in a supermarket, or you're feeling impatient at a stoplight, you can feel the answer internally. If you feel a pull toward sexually compulsive behavior, ask yourself what's always true. Then remember that you are not your mind, not your compulsions, but something more. Remembering what's always true will help you to stay in the moment so that you won't act in a negative way.

Again, you're not asking the question to get an answer, but to bring yourself back to conscious awareness. Your essence is in conscious awareness. The essential nature of you is found only in your conscious awareness. It's the aspect of you that knows exactly what to do at any time without long intellectual conversations or emotional wrestling matches with yourself. It's beyond your thoughts.

You are not your thoughts. You are not your stories. You are your essence.

If you want to experience that right now, take a few moments to allow your mind to rest. Take a deep breath, let it out, relax, and notice your surroundings. If you can do this even for a few seconds before your thoughts start up, you have begun to experience your essence.

Your True Addiction Is to Your Mind

As I mentioned earlier, your essential nature or essence is what you were born with. It's who you were before you began accumulating thousands of experiences, memories, and sensations. Can you imagine yourself as a baby lying in your crib? You can't talk, and you have no mental ability and no sense of reasoning. You just are. You look around and there are these people. You begin to see them more clearly, and they're giving you food—milk from a breast or a bottle. As you get older, they try to talk to you, moving their lips. You hear them and they're making cooing sounds. If you're lucky, they are people who love you.

As you get a little older, your intellect starts to form and you begin to have some reasoning ability. But you're still young and everything has to do with getting your needs met. You want to be fed. You want the breast or the bottle. You want a toy. As you get older, if you have good parents, they teach you, even as a young kid, to share your toys and to delay gratification. "Yes, you can have that tomorrow" becomes okay with you.

But maybe, instead, you're suffering because your parents aren't able to take care of you the way you need them to. Maybe they're drunk or screaming and you've been betrayed or abandoned. As a child, you have the sense that it's imperative that your needs are met. If there's no one there to help you meet your needs, you depend on whatever you see, taste, touch, and hear to help you cope and feel better.

Later, what makes you feel good might be seeing your mommy naked, or a bra ad, or sexy dancing on television. You may feel excited or not, but it's certainly different than feeling bad. You're too young to feel really sexual, but you feel something. The breast that fed you may now become the breast that you depend on to meet your voyeuristic needs. It may become essential to you that you get whatever it is that feels good to you.

It's important to those of us who are or were addicted to have our sexual satisfaction, our warmth, our secret lives. And some of us chose not to have it with real people. For men who were subjected to emotional incest by their mothers, during which their mothers may have acted in a sexually inappropriate way toward them, it makes some odd sense to use pornography. By using pornography, a man with this past experience knows very clearly that the women in the photos are not his mother, so there are no incestuous feelings when desiring them.

There are other men who prefer paying for sex or having one-night stands so that afterwards they won't have to talk to the person. Such a man might confuse sex with intimacy. In truth, he may have a lack of comfort and familiarity with intimacy, which extends to the postcoital conversation that often takes place between partners. If you feel a similar discomfort with intimacy, one reason could be that you were not taught about intimacy or didn't witness it in the home where you grew up.

In my case, the home where I grew up was where my mother walked around naked and, when I was six years old, starting paying me quarters to massage her breasts. I wanted attention from my mother, and her permission to be that intimate with her made me feel wanted and nurtured. I felt she was favoring me over my younger brother. Because my mother intruded into my personal life in a sexual way when I was a boy, I didn't separate myself from her in a healthy way, which was very confusing to me.

As an adult in recovery, I began to practice asking what's always true. When I had some experience with it, I could resist getting lost in my sexual compulsions by bringing myself back to me, to my essence. Since then it has been much easier for me to be with another person without confusing that person with my own fear, pain, shame, self-doubt, judgment, criticism, or anger, all of which used to ruin the intimate experience of sex.

Getting in touch with what's always true can enable you to stop the pull of compulsive behavior and be who you really are rather than who you think yourself to be.

Communicating with Your Complexes

If you're reading this book, you're most likely an adult who has had hundreds and thousands of experiences. From these thousands of experiences, you've built up stories. Some of these are true, some are not, and some are addictive. What I want you to do is to create a filter or a "go-to place" in your amphitheater so you'll know what to do when a voice demands that you should "Get porn!"

I want you to become your essence. I want you to find a real father, mentor, guide, or teacher within yourself. The goal of this book is that you will never have to read this or any other book on sex addiction again. If you become your essence, you'll be able to let the addicted voices of your past slide right on by. When the negative subpersonalities based on all of your old stories speak up—The Drinker, Porn Guy, Angry Guy, Fear Guy, The Shameful One—you will have another technique to counteract them.

As you become proficient with being silent and experiencing your essence, even for a few moments, you can then use your essential nature in your amphitheater to filter out subpersonalities, such as your addict self. I always recommend writing down your inner dialogues or conversations. After you're proficient at dialoging, you can do it in your mind as situations arise and subpersonalities speak up. Later, when your mind has changed, this process becomes automatic. What happens is that you begin to reform your thinking patterns so that you filter negative impulses through what's always true—your conscious awareness and essence. If you practice asking what's always true, you begin to behave in ways more congruent with your true self.

You never know when you might be triggered. It might be a whiff of perfume. It might be a flash of cleavage or thigh. You may never know when your sex addict will be aroused. But you can be prepared by being who you really are. The essence of you is in the amphitheater with the lights on. Then, when the impulse arises to act out sexually, your essence can respond, "No, no thanks. I don't want to do porn. That could be harmful."

If you keep practicing this, and especially if you write it all down, you will become the guy who does not do porn, who forgets to do porn, or the guy who can walk by a strip club and glance at the photos of the women without wishing that you could have these false girlfriends.

The Benefits of Stillness

Trying to be still is difficult. Nobody ever stays "awake" all the time. No one is constantly enlightened. For instance, take this story of a Buddhist monk. It's a joke I like to tell to my clients. The monk goes into the cave and he's in bliss for a whole week. He's got a shrine where he burns incense while he meditates all day. Every Saturday morning he comes out of the cave to get a little package of food that someone leaves for him. He looks down at the food and says, "Ah, shit—rice again."

Just because you're awake or consciously aware does not mean you'll have a blissful life. It just means that you'll get over your story quicker. Everyone reading this book is a human being blessed with unique and wonderful abilities. However, those positive attributes are often kept hidden by the intense drive to satiate what cannot be satiated. There aren't enough porn sites, strip clubs, prostitutes, massage parlors (or whatever your addiction) to make it so that you will have enough. You can never have enough of what won't satisfy you. You cannot be satiated. The people who sell porn know this and are skillful in their presentation. Once you stop listening to your mind's false tricks, you'll be able to find what does truly satisfy. You can begin to move beyond your mind and experience your essence.

EXERCISE: Tell Yourself What's Always True

This exercise is about getting in touch with what's always true—your essence, the essential nature of you. Find a quiet place with as few distractions as possible. Don't do this in a bar or a coffee shop. But you can be outside, walking in a park or looking at the mountains or the ocean. Take some deep breaths and really feel your breath. Most of the time your breathing is automatic. This time, consciously realize that you are breathing. The first time you do this, do it for three to five minutes. Then, as you become used to paying attention to your breath, do it for longer periods.

Feel the air as it moves through your lungs. Feel the blood flowing in your arms. Feel the breath going in and out of your lungs. Then take a few deeper breaths and just be quiet for a second to see what happens. Now try it again.

Mind will come in and say, "What're you doing? Stop this bullshit. You're a traitor," "This breathing stuff is for New Agers or meditators. I'm not a fucking monk," "Let's forget this and go masturbate." That's your mind. You know that now. You can stop it. You can sink down below your mind into your breath, your essence. This moment is for you. You don't need anything or anyone else. You don't need porn in this moment. You're having a few seconds of relief from the constant chatter of your mind. Being still and paying attention to your breath is a way to refresh and recharge yourself.

Your mind will bring up excuses: "I'm too busy for this shit," or "I've got more important things to do." If you find your thoughts wandering, don't judge or criticize. Just realize that this is a process. I've gone through it, and I've seen hundreds of people like you go through it. Mind is a worthy adversary. Mind will constantly want you to pay attention to your old script, going from one story to the next and to the next, all day and all night. Your true addiction is to your mind. But you are not your mind. Continue to ask yourself, "What's always true?," and trust the process.

All of my clients have objected to doing this exercise. But you've done stranger things. You've done things that hurt you. You've done things that hurt other people. Now try something that could make you more relaxed and make it easier for you to always know who you are, to always know that you are more than your constant thoughts about sex, and that you are the one in charge. If you do this, the positive results may spill over into your work, your relationships, and your life in general. You will be calmer and more self-assured because you'll really be in touch with yourself and what's always true.

I will tell you one more time what's always true: the answers to your life problems are so close—they're in the silence of what's always true. Your entire experience of being alive can change. If bad or difficult things happen and you feel a pull toward acting out in a sexually compulsive way, you won't have to do it. All you'll need to do is to ask yourself, "What's always true?"

The next chapter describes a technique for being aware of when your addict subpersonality is taking control.

CHAPTER 6

The Blonde in the Beemer:
What to Do When You're Out of Control

Sometimes it's difficult to know when your addict self is in control. In fact, you may be driving down the road, feeling fine, and run headlong into an addictive stranglehold. This chapter will help you recognize when you're heading down this road and give you the tools to take the next exit.

The Blond in the BMW

Some years ago, before I had broken the stranglehold of sex addiction, I was driving north on California Highway 101 toward Salinas, which is south of San Francisco. I had a tendency then, as now, to drive a hot car and cruise over the speed limit. At that time, I didn't have a radar detector. My typical tactic was to tail a trucker who was going faster than the limit. If there was a highway patrol officer hiding up ahead, he'd tag the trucker first. However, on this particular day, there were no trucks.

Then I saw the blonde in the Beemer.

At that time, a significant percentage of my day was spent fantasizing, spinning elaborate sexual scenarios. When I saw the beautiful blonde hair, my fantasy spinner began to go full tilt. The blonde was doing 70 in a 55 mile-an-hour zone. "I'll just tuck in behind her," I thought. "If there's a speed trap, she'll get caught and I can keep going."

I started fixating on that long blonde hair and that car. Wow! It was a shiny, new, red, top-of-the-line BMW. She must be beautiful and have money. By now, my sexual-compulsion fantasy spinner was also doing 70 miles per hour.

Wow! My lucky day. I get to speed through the valley and finally realize my long-standing fantasy of a beautiful woman driver wanting to hook up with me. My mind was spinning. "Man, it would be nice to have somebody like that. She's probably not just beautiful, but maybe even fashion-model beautiful. I wonder how big her breasts are."

We kept racing along 101, the sex addict in my head talking nonstop. "I wonder if she's looking in the rear-view mirror and thinking about me. Maybe she's thinking she's getting turned on by driving fast and would love to pull over and fuck somebody—like the guy following her. "

There was a work project I needed to think through. But I didn't want to think about that. I even turned off the car radio just so I could totally focus on the fantasy about the blonde in the Beemer. The air conditioner was going full blast, but I was still perspiring. My hand even went into my pocket, and I wasn't looking for my Swiss Army knife.

I kept my car right behind hers because I was so into the fantasy about this woman I wished I could have right that instant. And I really believed she might pull over and give me oral sex.

Do You Know When You're Out of Control?

I'll finish this story in a minute. Right now I want you to ask yourself: How many times has your fantasy world taken over reality? What percentage of your day is spent thinking about sex and how to get it? If you don't know the answer, stop for even ten seconds and consider how much of your time is spent chasing your version of what I've labeled the "Blonde in the Beemer."

When I was on 101, following the blonde in the Beemer, this fantasy went on and on. I drove for twenty, thirty, then forty miles, all the while fantasizing about driving by and waving. The fantasy had gotten me so turned on that I thought about masturbating even while going 70 miles an hour and passing a lot of other cars. Disregarding reality, I started to rub myself, even though I was endangering not only myself but others. You may have your own story like this one. I've heard stories that were much more extreme. As sex addicts, we do crazy things.

Finally, her turn signal started blinking. I was so far into this fantasy with the blonde that I had lost touch with where I was on the 101. I even interpreted the blink of her directional light as a signal directed at me.

Next, I watched as she began to slow down in preparation to take the turn ahead onto another road. To my surprise, I realized that she wasn't looking in the rear-view mirror. I saw that she wasn't even looking at me, let alone motioning for me to follow her. I was so far into the fantasy that I thought, "I better pull alongside so she'll see me and maybe motion to me."

Before she started the turn, I gunned the engine and pulled up alongside her. I glanced to my right, expecting to finally see the face of the object of my, by now, almost hour-long fantasy. But all I saw was the oily-looking, acne-scarred face of an unattractive middle-aged man who happened to have long blonde hair.

Your Behavior Is a Wake-Up Call— Pay Attention!

Seeing that blond-haired man in the BMW was like having the heavyweight champion of the world punch me in the solar plexus. I felt dizzy and almost as if I had to puke. This event was a major wake-up call for me. I had not only spent an hour on this crazy fantasy, but I had put my life in danger and possibly jeopardized the lives of other drivers, only to realize I had been following one butt-ugly guy. In fact, my eyes were finally opened to the fact that I wasted a good deal of my life on wishing, wondering, and fantasizing.

What about you? Have you wasted time and possibly endangered yourself or your family? Maybe you could be caught by your wife, by the police, or even by your children. Maybe you could have caught an STD, even AIDS. Think again about what percentage of your day is spent thinking of sex and how to get it. It could be time spent looking at porn on the computer, but it doesn't have to be. It could be at the grocery store, at the health club, or in line at the movies. You could be thinking about porn, prostitutes, strippers, or affairs. I calculate that during the time I was acting out sexually, I lost over a million dollars in wages by focusing on the equivalent of the "Blonde in the Beemer," the fantasy rather than reality.

You did not pick up this book because your sex life is the norm. You probably picked it up because you spend a lot of time fantasizing. Now ask yourself: are you going to wake up before you have an "accident," such as getting caught, getting mugged, losing your money, getting beaten up by a pimp, or losing your job?

Don't kid yourself. You are endangering not only yourself but others. Even though your wife or girlfriend or children don't know the details of your fantasies or your actions, your behavior still impacts them. For example, I was so caught up in my sexual compulsion that I was not really present for my first two wives. When I had sex with my first or second wife, I was thinking about the latest stripper I'd seen or the check-out girl at the food store. I was thinking about people with whom I had no relationship, just as I obviously had no relationship with the blonde in the Beemer. My fantasies meant I was out of touch with the real people in my life. And that cost me not only time and relationships, but intimacy and love.

My first two marriages did not end just because I was a sex addict. They ended in divorce because I did not show up in the relationship. That's how I was when I was tailing the blonde in the Beemer. I was not really there. I was not really in my car on that road. I was lost in a fantasy world far, far away from real life.

This chapter is about learning how to wake up when your addict becomes lost following the Blonde in the Beemer in your life. Here's my own example of a follow-up dialogue with my addict after the episode I always refer to as the Blonde in the Beemer.

George: That was a *guy* in that Beemer! An ugly guy!

Addict: I don't want to talk about it. It could have been a blonde. And, she could have wanted to have sex with you.

George: Are you kidding? This is crazy! You need to stop doing this. You need to convert your energy into positive adult thinking and behavior.

Addict: But it's always been like this. You need me.

George: For what? You are acting like a child. A needy child. You somehow got stuck in this behavior— objectifying and sexualizing women. I'm a man now, and this is silly. Especially since you do it all the time and I end up masturbating to porn.

Addict: What's so bad about that? We're not hurting anyone.

George: What's so bad? I'm alone. I'm afraid of real intimacy with a real, live woman. I want to love and be loved. Yeah, it's scary to even think about it, but I deserve it.

I did and do deserve real intimacy—and so do you. And the only way to get it is to move beyond the fantasy and dive into the reality that's waiting for you.

From Fantasy to Intimacy

Does my Blonde in the Beemer story resonate with you? Have you spent hours chasing your own fantasies? Yes? I thought so. That's the reason I shared this crazy episode with you. Maybe you even laughed at my misadventure. But then you saw how it applied to your life. Fantasy addiction is a way to "leave" yourself, leave what is real, and pretend you're going to have a sexual experience that truly satisfies you. But instead of having a real and satisfying encounter, you end up chasing the wrong person, staring at porn, or streaming video on your computer and pretending that it's you who is having the sex. How strange is that behavior? You can even have sex with a prostitute and still feel alone, because you *are* emotionally alone.

What if you could go from fantasy to intimacy? What if you could change so that, instead of fantasies about porn stars you'll never meet or prostitutes that don't care about you, you get greater satisfaction with a real woman with whom you are intimately sharing your life? Maybe that thought isn't appealing right now. Maybe you'd even admit that it scares you a little. After all, it seems much safer to have impersonal sex or just masturbate while you imagine having sex. The truth is, you can change. I did it. I've worked with hundreds of men who have done it. And changing from fantasy to intimacy has the highest payoff you could ever imagine.

One thing you need to be aware of is that you'll no longer get the same high or spiky rush that you might get now from your acting-out behavior. But you also won't have the shame and misery that often follows the high. What you can get after breaking free of sexually compulsive behavior is a nice, steady buzz of intimacy and connection. When you go home to the same loving partner every night, you get to experience a real sense of connection with another, and when you're alone, your connection with yourself isn't swamped by the guilt and shame of your acting-out behavior.

Right now you're on the losing end. It's no secret that sex sells. As long as the porn industry, the prostitutes, and the strip clubs feed your fantasies, you keep feeding their bank accounts. It's not the same as buying a car and keeping it for a year or more. Your fantasies need to be fed over and over again—weekly, daily, or even hourly. The people getting the payoff are the ones taking your cash. And you're left alone and ultimately unsatisfied because you keep needing to feed your compulsion over and over. You're in a vicious cycle. The good news is that you can break that cycle. You can get the real payoff. You can go from fantasy to intimacy.

■ Craig's Harem Fantasy

Craig had always wanted a lot of girls—a harem or stable of women. He wasn't bad looking, but he had never been the tall, handsome kind of guy who easily charmed the opposite sex. He met his intelligent, attractive wife on a blind date and now they have children. But he never lost that fantasy of having a lot of women.

Craig joined a website for men who pay to be "supportive" sugar daddies for younger women. He communicated with a woman who replied that she was working her way through college. This woman, whom we'll call Tanya, had paid the sugar daddy website to feed her contacts of men who would give her what the website called an "allowance." In return for paying the allowance, Craig was entitled to have sex with Tanya once every two weeks. After Craig paid the fee and met Tanya, he had doubts about whether she was actually a student. But, for Craig, it was the fantasy that mattered, and Tanya was the first member in his stable of women. Next, he would find two or three similar women to support and he'd be on his way to achieving his fantasy goal.

Having a lot of sexually available women was Craig's Blonde in the Beemer. The fantasy consumed his thoughts, and he looked at photos of women for hours on the website for sugar-daddy wannabes. When not at the computer, he spent more time planning how his fantasy would play out. Although financially feasible, the cost would put a severe strain on his budget. But Craig figured that he could always tap into his savings and his IRA if he needed to. After all, his addictive thinking led him to believe that he'd been a good husband and father and was therefore entitled to whatever would make him happy. Craig didn't want to think about the reality. After all, if his wife found out, it would poison their marriage. She would divorce him and he would no longer live with her and the two children he adored. He would be relegated to visitation privileges, if he was lucky.

After Craig began working with me, I told him my *Blonde in the Beemer* story. Although he initially tried to deny any resemblance the story had to his own life, he soon realized that he was living in a dangerous fantasy world. What usually works to break the stranglehold of addictive fantasies is to have the person who is chasing his or her *Blonde in the Beemer* do the equivalent of what I did when I drove up next to the car. I clearly saw the reality, and the fantasy was shattered.

In Craig's case, that fantasy was having a stable of women and what that would mean to him and about him. We first worked on demystifying the word "stable." It's the word that Craig used most often, and it triggered his flights into fantasy. Demystifying the word entails looking at what the word or thought symbolizes. When he was a teenager, Craig had read men's magazine articles about having a stable of women. This had stuck with him, especially since in high school and college it was difficult for him to have even one woman in his life. It took Craig several weeks of using the dialogue technique to demystify the word "stable" so it was no longer a trigger for his fantasy. That's when he completely understood that his fantasy of wanting a stable was accomplishing nothing except to "de-stabilize" the rest of his life. Here's an example of Craig's dialogue:

Craig: You seem to be hard at work in there.

Addict Craig: Yes, I am.

Craig: Why?

Addict Craig: Life is too stressful. We need to get back to porn and having affairs. Take our mind off things.

Craig:	You know where that leads.
Addict Craig:	At least we don't have to deal with stress, though.
Craig:	It has been pretty tough to quiet our mind.
Addict Craig:	Yes, and why fight it? You don't have to quiet it. We can just do something fun and it will quiet down itself.
Craig:	Part of me wishes we could. But doing something "fun" is really just doing something leading to long-term destruction.
Addict Craig:	Well, let's deal with that another day.
Craig:	Another day is today. We can't put this off. We both know it. We have to continually work at this. Taking an hour, a day, a week off is just more lost time, and that much longer until we can start being normal—or at least as close to normal as we can.
Addict Craig:	I don't like it.
Craig:	Sometimes I don't, either. But we need to be responsible. Doesn't sound as fun as porn and the prospect of screwing hot girls and having a stable of them. But those aren't any fun in the long run anyway. Quite the opposite.
Addict Craig:	Who cares.

Craig:	We both know that not dealing with life is not a viable option.
Addict Craig:	So what?
Craig:	Help me quiet our mind down. I know that it's you running around inside, and it feels like my head is going to explode.
Addict Craig:	That's because you're not listening to me.
Craig:	Help me deal with this shit. We need to face life head-on. It may be tough at times, but I know it'll be okay. Actually, much more than okay.

Craig was able to disentangle himself from his fantasy, discontinue his sugar-daddy membership, and sever his relationship with Tanya.

Crashing Fantasy with Reality

In examples in this chapter, both Craig and I chased our fantasies. But where did our fantasies originate? As I mentioned, in high school Craig read men's magazine articles about having a stable of women. He imagined having that stable for himself, particularly when he had difficulty getting even one woman to date. Most of us have similar experiences where we hear, read, or see something that leads to a fantasy.

Similarly, boys and young men in school and college talk about how exciting it is to "get a lot of pussy" or "make it with the cheerleader." When we're adults, a part of us knows that the excitement is mostly based on the fantasy. But that's the point. The fantasies are something you started believing when you were a kid, like you should eat a lot of candy because it tastes so wonderful. As you got older, you realized you didn't want to eat a lot of candy. All that sugar would rot your teeth and you actually don't feel so good when you eat too much candy. So you matured and said to yourself that you'd eat candy once in a while.

Now imagine a fantasy woman you probably already spend a lot of your time thinking about. She's like the candy you wanted too much of when you were a kid. In your fantasy, she's exactly as you want her to be, just as you may have imagined it would be like to go out with that sexy cheerleader in high school. But what if, in reality, she had a personality that was real? What if she could be difficult and demanding? What if her breath smelled odd? Or her stomach constantly growled? Or one breast was slightly smaller than the other? Or she had pimples on her butt?

Your fantasy is not real. That's why you can never truly have your fantasy. That's why, now that you're an adult, it's time to let go of the fantasies. The fantasy of having amazing sex with lots of beautiful women who want nothing more than to adore you is like eating candy without thinking about the reality. And eye candy does not make for intimacy. It has a momentary pleasure, like putting chocolate in your mouth, but then it's gone. I personally love chocolate, but as soon as it hits my stomach, I have to digest it and it probably turns into fat. That's not good.

When I was younger, I had sex with many beautiful women. It was the same thing every time, just like eating chocolate. When I was done, I actually didn't feel so good. Physical beauty does not make for a relationship. On the other hand, if you spend time with a person you have a strong connection with or have interests in common with, then being sexual with that person can leave you feeling extremely good.

I realize that it can be difficult for a man to think with his big head rather than his little one. I've been there. And I'm asking you to stop for a second and give yourself a chance to make a decision based on what, in the long run, is best for you, your life, and your family. Think with your heart instead of with your addict's mind. The addict is going to keep telling you that your sexually compulsive behavior is what you need to do.

If you've read the preceding chapters, you know now that you don't have to listen to your addict. Now you also know that what your addict wants is a fantasy. It won't work. The truth is that you can't get enough of what won't satisfy you. Chasing your Blonde in the Beemer won't satisfy you. Imagining having sex with the woman you airbrush to perfection in your mind won't satisfy you.

Remember the guys talking in high school about banging the cheerleaders, or the centerfolds, or the models? Sadly, no one talks about what is really satisfying, which is to date a regular person who hasn't been airbrushed, hold them, love them, kiss them, connect, and have deep, fulfilling, rich sex. So the woman is not a centerfold or a model. Are you? Have you been in any fashion magazine advertisements? Underwear ads? Have you looked in the mirror lately without your clothes on?

EXERCISE: Stop Chasing the Blonde in the Beemer

When you find yourself chasing your Blonde in the Beemer, or your stable of women, or the prostitute, stripper, or chat-room girl who you think is going to give you want you want, I want you to remember my story and Craig's story. Remember that both Craig and I had dialogues with our addict subpersonalities. You can do that, too. It's time to have a talk with the part of you that's screwing up your life—the guy in the soap opera who is always causing trouble. He's the addict who's taking your valuable time and demanding that you do something that's going to end up making you feel terrible. If you can write down your conversation with your addict, it will be more effective.

This is an opportunity to begin to change your behavior. This would be a time when you could name this subpersonality, this complex, and *anchor in* (as you would anchor in a boat) the realization that this is not who you are. It is a figment of your imagination, a figment of your fantasy. It's an aspect that is no longer useful, even though it promises you that, beyond any doubt, you will feel wonderful. Afterwards, you'll sit there in your dark room, in your misery, with the equivalent of a handful of glue, saying, "Oh shit— I've done it again. Now I'm late for work." Or "I should've been home an hour ago. What am I going to tell my wife?"

This is also the time when you make excuses. You're upset and you promise yourself that you'll never let it happen again—until tomorrow or the next day. Because, until you have a talk, a dialogue, with the part of you that promises you'll feel better, it *will* happen, again, and again, and again. If you put off this dialogue, you'll succumb again to the addict's will, and you may end up paying a terrible price. It may be the loss of your job, your marriage, or your children, and it could be financial or legal trouble. It's time to stop. It's time to stop chasing the Blonde in the Beemer.

So, do this exercise and have that talk with your negative addict subpersonality. Talk to that aspect of yourself, that actor in your mind, that person in the amphitheater. Turn the lights on and say, "Hey, Porn Guy, Beemer Guy, Stripper Lover, here we are again. We've got to stop doing this. We've got to stop *now*." Let them tell you why you shouldn't stop. See if they make any sense. Then do something that actually does make sense rather than listening to your addict.

In the next chapter, you'll read about how and why you may have started down the road to sexually compulsive behavior and how you can find a new path to follow.

CHAPTER 7

Where You Hurt the Most: *Your Original Emotional Wound*

Wh* you build a house, you start with a foundation. If the foundation is not solid, the house could fall apart. If you're a golfer, you need a strong foundation, maybe a good swing, to excel. If no one taught you how to swing a golf club, you're not likely to be very good at the game. If you're a salesman, you require a strong foundation in how to convince people that they need a certain product or service. If no one taught you those skills and you never learned them on your own, your foundation as a salesperson will be faulty. It's the same with your life. You need to start with a strong foundation.

When you looked at your history, particularly your childhood, you were looking at your foundation. That's what your life is built on. If people were kind and loving with you, if they taught you how to be intimate with others and how to build and sustain a friendship, then you have a strong foundation for forming loving relationships. If that teaching was lacking, you very likely have problems with your foundation. You're going to have the emotional equivalent of concrete that didn't set right: weak spots and fractures. One particular aspect of your foundation has had a massive impact on your life. That huge influence would be your original emotional wound.

What Is an Original Emotional Wound?

An *original emotional wound*, or just original wound, always begins in childhood, and it can remain open and unhealed well into adult life. Although it sounds similar, it has no connection with what some religions refer to as original sin. "A particular behavior…presses on an old wound, triggering a response in us that is clearly an overreaction. This is perhaps the site of the original wound" (Dayton 2000, 21).

The original wound is an event that has left an emotional hurt that has not healed. It need not be related to sex or sexual activity, although it impacts nearly every interaction with members of the opposite sex (or same sex, if you are gay or lesbian). People who have suffered such original wounds spend their adult lives responding and reacting to new circumstances in exactly the same way that they reacted and responded when the original wound was first received, even though their life circumstances may be entirely different.

Moreover, the original wound has a great deal to do with determining the kind of coping behavior people put into place to deal with their wounds. Compulsive sexual behavior is almost always a coping mechanism created specifically to deal with the original wound. In my experience, when you explore your history and see your original wound through adult eyes, you can begin to resolve or heal it. When you are no longer reacting to the original wound, your sexually compulsive behavior can change.

Notice the Contradictions in Your Life

If you're a football player in the United States, you need to learn how to catch a pass. If there's a problem with your concentration, you might miss the pass or drop it. That can happen when there's a contradiction in your actions between catching a pass, wanting to get over the first-down marker, and being a bit fearful of the two-hundred-and-fifty-pound linebacker who is about to collide with you. If you're looking toward the goal line rather than at the football as it approaches your outstretched hands, you could easily drop the pass or miss it altogether. In other words, when your focus is split, you won't make a very good wide receiver because you'll drop too many passes.

Now imagine the football player is you in your relationships. For example, suppose you're married but you still want to have sex with two or three different women every week. That's a contradiction that won't lead to a successful, intimate marriage. Now that you've looked back at your history while reading chapters 2 and 4, I want you to focus on the original wound that may have created the contradiction in your actions.

Your Original Wound Is Like an Injury

You might think of your original wound as being similar to the injury of an athlete with a torn knee ligament. Even when the knee is repaired and the player goes through rehabilitation, he may still be more susceptible to injury in the place where that original wound occurred. In addition, the original wound could hold him back. He's afraid of reinjuring it and may not play to the best of his ability. That's his story. That's his belief—that the knee could easily be reinjured. As a result, he may mentally limit or handicap himself on the playing field and perhaps in life.

Although the original wound I want you to discover is emotional rather than physical, the point is to see how that original emotional wound was your reaction to a situation or event in your life. Once you see the original wound for what it is, you can change your perception of it and no longer allow it to cripple your life. Uncovering your original wound can enable you to free yourself from the contradictions that result in compulsive behaviors.

■ *Bill and the Cheerleader*

As a high-school student, Bill was afraid to ask a girl if she wanted to see a movie with him. On game day, he watched a particular cheerleader and wanted to ask her out. But Bill wasn't on the football team and didn't have the courage to even talk to her. He was a regular kid, but he believed he was defective. Either he was too short, or he had pimples, or he was too thin. As a result of his belief, he was afraid of girls. He didn't know what to do. He had poor role modeling from his mother and father, who weren't affectionate with each other or with their son. No one ever talked to him about girls or sex.

In this simplified example, Bill's original wound was low self-esteem, and as an adult, he was still afraid to talk to a woman. But if Bill was looking at women on the Internet, or paying them at strip clubs, he didn't have to fear being turned down. As a way to cope with his fear—his crippling belief that he didn't know how to talk to a woman—Bill developed sexually compulsive behaviors.

■ *Keith and Multiple Cheerleaders*

Keith also developed sexually compulsive behavior. However, Keith was almost the reverse of Bill. Keith was handsome and self-assured with women. Yet Keith also had an original wound that had to do with girls and sex. Remember the example of the handsome twelve-year-old boy with the nonexistent home life who was seduced by his sixteen-year-old cheerleader babysitter? That was Keith. He received very little parenting from his mom and dad. Keith's father was a functioning alcoholic who was not able to really be there as a father figure. Keith's mother kept her husband at a distance and, although they stayed together, Keith didn't grow up seeing a way for men and women to be intimate, close, or even great friends. As a result, Keith's babysitter represented all of what intimacy and love were supposed to be.

Because of the dysfunction in his household and his early sexual experience, Keith picked sex as a coping strategy. Keith had sex with a lot of cheerleaders and other women, but it was never enough to recapture the feeling he had when he was twelve. It was just never enough to quench his inner longing. Even after marrying, Keith continued having sex with prostitutes. Like Bill, Keith picked sex as a coping strategy.

Dialogue to Convert Negative Behavior to Positive

From preceding chapters, you should have a good idea of how to dialogue with your addict subpersonality. Here's an abbreviated but real-life example from the client called Keith in the example above. He calls his addict subpersonality "Hotshot."

Hotshot: We should get a little pussy.

Keith: No, we're married.

Hotshot: But we can have anything we want.

Keith: We did that years ago.

Hotshot: Fuck that. You're wasting your time and your money. You're a player, and if you're a player, you should play.

Keith: Well, we can't do that anymore. We'd end up getting another divorce. We've been divorced twice now.

Hotshot: Who cares? Just don't bother getting married.

Keith: I want intimacy.

Hotshot: Intimacy is a bunch of crap. It's an illusion. It's not as good as pussy.

From reading what he wrote in this dialogue and others, Keith more clearly saw the ferocity of his addict self and how that part of him wanted to take him away from his marriage. He reaffirmed how much he loved his wife and did not want to lose the marriage. By dialoguing, Keith was able to begin breaking away from his story and from living in reaction to his addict self. He was able to begin to see and heal his original emotional wound. Once you expose your original wound to the light of day, you can begin to free yourself from living in reaction to your history.

Let's listen in on Keith and Hotshot again for a brief example of how Keith's dialogues evolved.

Keith: Hotshot, how would you like to convert your energy into skydiving, bike riding, or having real intimacy?

Hotshot: Do you think that's possible?

Keith:	Of course it is.
Hotshot:	I'm afraid to do that.
Keith:	Just trust me and trust the process we're doing here.
Hotshot:	Okay. I'll try.

If, like Keith, you engage in dialogues with your addict self on a regular basis, you can change how your mind works about sexually compulsive behavior. Your nicknamed character can assume a new identity or evolve into a whole new character.

Are you ready to delve deeper into your personal history, uncover your original wound, stop the bleeding, and resolve the emotional pain? Are you ready to be who you were meant to be? Just like Keith, you can confront the part of you that is still living in reaction to your original wound. You can change the addict self who is still trying to make up for what didn't happen, help you cope with the shame and fear you no longer need, or help you to stop hopelessly trying to recapture the highs of early sexual experiences.

Addiction as a Reaction to Your Original Wound

Just to be clear, the original wound doesn't have to be sexual in nature. What an individual did or does in reaction to the original wound (his or her coping behavior), though, is what can become sexually compulsive behavior.

In my counseling practice, I've seen a lot of clients whose wounds involved a lack of intimacy. That is, they grew up without witnessing intimacy in parental relationships in early home life.

However, the original wound can come from many diverse negative childhood experiences.

By finding your original wound—whatever it may be and whenever it occurred—you too can find freedom from sexually compulsive behavior. As we know, one very effective technique is to write a dialogue with your addict self. If you write such a dialogue and set it aside for a few minutes, then read it over, you may gain some insight into how and why your addict subpersonality is constantly driving you toward sexually compulsive behavior.

■ *Ryan's Original Wound: The World of Pretend*

In chapter 4, I described Ryan as growing up in a family where his father pretended that they were better off financially than they were. The father inflated the family's status. One reason there was no reality or intimacy in the home was that the constant effort to keep up the charade prevented any real closeness. Ryan's original wound was living a lie and the distance that put between him and every member of his family. Even as a child, it was clear to Ryan that the emperor (his father) had no clothes. But a child cannot confront his parents about living a lie. A child needs his parents for food, shelter, and whatever love he can get. So Ryan got along as best he knew how—and he was seriously wounded.

In order to uncover the connection between his original wound and his sexually compulsive behavior, Ryan wrote a dialogue between his adult self and the wounded boy. In another step in the healing process, Ryan formed a connection with a deeper part of himself, his essential self—the core part of himself that was not tied to a specific personality or issue or story. As you work with the techniques you learned

in chapter 5, you, too, can be more at one with this core,
essential part of yourself. Ryan was able to convert his
wounded boy into an adult man who was no longer at the
mercy of his addict personality.

Compulsive Behavior and Shame

Many original wounds have an element of shame. In the United
States, there has always been a puritanical influence on sexual
attitudes, and that tone can be strengthened by the views of
many religious institutions. In the case of sex addiction, needing
to engage in sexually compulsive behavior can lead to feeling even
more shame and guilt. Whatever your original wound is, it likely
involves an element of shame.

Gays and lesbians in our culture have been particularly vulnerable to being wounded early on by shame. Kids and teens who are
perceived as gay are all too often subjected to unmerciful shaming.
In many instances, young boys who recognize themselves as gay
also have fathers who want their sons to be manly in conventional
terms. Such a father might try to force the boy to engage in tra-
ditionally masculine pursuits, such as sports, and possibly boast
about his heterosexual exploits. If the boy feels no affinity for
these kinds of activities, the message is sent that he is less than
masculine—and less than okay. These types of situations can lead
to a common original wound among children whose parents will
not let them be who they really are.

This wound is called *internalized homophobia* and refers to a
negative feeling toward oneself because of homosexuality. Because
most children who grow up in the United States "internalize soci-
etal heterosexism from an early age...lesbians and gay men usually
experience some degree of negative feeling toward themselves
when they first recognize their own homosexuality in adolescence

or adulthood. This sense of what is usually called internalized homophobia often makes the process of identity formation more difficult" (Herek et al. 1997, 17).

Although this section focused on the blatant shame that is instilled in many gay men and lesbians, every one of my clients has had an element of shame connected with his or her sexuality and subsequent acting-out behaviors.

EXERCISE: The Unsent Letter

One valuable technique for dealing with compulsive sex addiction is to write an unsent letter to your parents or primary caregivers. This letter could be angry, sad, happy, indifferent, joyful, contrite, or vindictive. The only requirement is that the letter expresses how you truly feel. If you write while aware of your original wound, you may experience relief from the pressure of the wounding. If you had a father who yelled at you, this is your opportunity to talk back. If you had an uncle who abused you and your parents wouldn't listen, this is your chance to express your anger toward your parents for not protecting you.

In writing the unsent letter, the theme of parental betrayal is common. Many people more clearly see the theme of shame in their childhood. The point is to write about your past so that you can see it, taste it, feel it, and ultimately move beyond it. This is one way that we can begin to understand our history and the story we have believed about ourselves.

Once you see and understand your story and your original wound, you will be able to see how that story impacts your behavior today. You can then decide whether or not you want to keep the story, your original wound, and your behavior. You are then empowered to move beyond your story.

Here is a version of what one client wrote about his original wound in his unsent letter:

"Dad, I don't understand why you thought that keeping your porn in a drawer made it a secret. By the time I was six years old, I had found your porn. I developed a habit of looking at it and becoming aroused. I didn't think it was bad. On the contrary, I thought if my daddy was doing it, it had to be good. It was Daddy's secret, so it must be exciting. It must be wonderful. But then something bad happened.

"Mommy caught me with your porn and I was sent to my room without dinner. Then I heard you and Mommy arguing. Later, you barged into my room and spanked me for looking at your porn. I think you were really mad at me because mommy didn't know about your porn until she found me looking at it.

"So she was angry at you and you were angry at me. But I didn't understand that then. Mommy stopped speaking to you and told me that you were a dirty old man. But I was only six years old! How could I have been prepared to hear what you said to me or what Mommy said about you? How could I have understood that it wasn't really my fault?

"For me, it was a shock to my six-year-old emotional and nervous systems. It was like I had post-traumatic stress disorder at six! Now I finally understand how what happened then became my original wound. And, Dad, it's time for me to grow up now and convert the negative, regressive energy from this wound into positive self-esteem and adult behavior."

_____

After you write a letter, you can keep it or perform a sort of destruction ritual. You might even burn the letter to symbolize your freedom from the feelings you expressed in the letter. What

I have sometimes done is put the letter in an envelope labeled "Dad," for example, with no address or return address. I put on a stamp and drop the letter into a blue mailbox. When I hear the "clunk" of the mailbox slot, I feel more complete.

EXERCISE: Look for Your Original Wound

Remember that, when looking for your original wound, it could be buried in a hidden part of your personality. For example, it could be in the way that you feel not good enough. Consequently, you're afraid to ask a woman out because you don't want to tell her you're a plumber, or a schoolteacher, or an accountant. You think that if you were a multimillionaire you would feel more confident, though that's not necessarily true. Your belief that you are less-than or not good enough originates not in what you do but in who you think you are. In other words, you perceive that this inadequacy lies at the very heart of who you are. This could be your original wound.

Find a quiet place to sit alone by yourself. Search through your history and inside yourself for what fits for you as an original wound. Allow yourself as much time as you need. If you have difficulty finding it, here are some additional steps to take:

- Pay attention to the feeling you have when you want to engage in compulsive behavior, and ask yourself: "When was the first time I felt this feeling?"

- Relax, let the world slip away, and drop deeper into your feelings. Drop down into a quiet place inside where you experience your deepest relaxation, acceptance, and peacefulness. This is your essence, a deeper part of yourself that I introduced in chapter 5.

- Ask yourself: "Am I ready to be who I was really meant to be, before the early wounding? What do I have to do to get there?"

- Look at the various pieces of the puzzle of your life— everything that has happened in your life—and start to put the pieces together in a new way using what you've learned so far. The clues are inside you. They are there for you to find.

Now that you are clearer about the role of your original wound in your story, we'll explore how to take another step beyond your story and your addictive behavior.

CHAPTER 8

Break the Cycle of Self-Blame: *Stepping Beyond Your Story*

You may think you are being very independent and making self-determining decisions every day. Most of us feel that way. But almost everything you do, everything you think, everything that happens to you is filtered through what you've done before, felt before, and experienced before. As I explained in chapter 1, we are all living in reaction to our histories. However, most of those prior experiences have nothing to do with sexually compulsive behavior and are actually quite useful.

Maybe you drink five glasses of water a day because you have a story about it being good for you. Or maybe you wear certain clothes without thinking because the story around them is that they signify success. You automatically stop at red lights without even thinking because you have a story about them, too. You may see doing this as "the law," and you believe that it's good and right to follow the law. You behave in a similar way around your sexuality. You have a story about your compulsive behaviors, and most of the time you act as if it were the law, without even thinking about it. I want you to become aware that you have unconscious, automatic behavior that you do in reaction to the story you have about your sexuality. I want you to become aware that you have stories, and one story involves self-blame.

Coping Behaviors to Feel Better

The story you have could be connected with what made you feel better as a child when you were alone in your room and heard your parents arguing, or when your older brother was mean to you, or when your father gave you a beating. As a result of early life experiences, you may have developed a story that had to do with betrayal or abandonment or abuse.

My story was about my mother's sexually inappropriate behavior with me. I developed a story around sexuality before I was old enough to really understand sex or intimacy. As a result, for many years as an adult, I sought sex that was impersonal. Only when I had revealed my story was I able to embrace true sexuality and intimacy. Revealing the part of my story where I mistakenly blamed myself helped me free myself from my sexually compulsive behavior.

There are many examples of a person developing a story around sexuality before he was older and more emotionally stable than he was as a child. Your thoughts about sex could have started when your older sister insisted that she show you her breasts when you were six years old. A neighbor boy might have asked if you wanted to masturbate together. An uncle might have touched you inappropriately. What impact could these or similar occurrences have on a young child? As adults, we know what is inappropriate. But what does a child know about experiences like these?

In psychology, there is a theory about childhood development called *object relations*. Research in this area has shown that children do not blame those on whom they are dependent for food, shelter, and love. Instead, they blame themselves. Object relations theory was pioneered in the 1940s and '50s by British psychologists Ronald Fairbairn, D. W. Winnicott, and Harry Guntrip (Hamilton 2006). As a result of their studies with abused children, the British psychologists concluded that, prior to puberty, children do not yet have the maturity to understand what is happening to them. Specifically, they are not yet mature enough to place blame where it may belong, such as on the person they are depending on for food, shelter, and love. Instead, the child creates a story about it being his or her fault (Fairbairn et al. 2006).

Self-Blame: It Must Be Me

You're probably familiar with the situation of a wife who is beaten by her husband but blames herself. The husband claims he wouldn't have to do this if she had only done something different (cooked better, cleaned the house, spoken up, or kept quiet, for example). The wife feels responsible for her husband getting angry and beating her. Even as an adult, she blames herself. This self-blaming behavior probably began earlier, most likely in childhood. Just as there is no excuse for a husband beating his wife, there is no excuse for a parent abusing a child. Yet children often blame themselves.

As a child, you can be hurt or influenced negatively by your parents or other adults, but you believe you need them for your survival. The option to leave home does not occur to you. If, as a child, you were abused or mistreated, it's highly unlikely that you would contact Child Protective Services and ask to be placed in a foster home. So what do you do instead? In their research, the British psychologists discovered that a child in these situations tends to internalize his or her anger, fear, and shame. Instead of directing it toward the parent on whom he or she is dependent, the child keeps it within himself or herself. What you can't project out toward your parents, you turn in toward yourself. The child thinks, "It must be me." Even if the child is getting beaten or raped, a child will think, "Mommy or Daddy can't be bad. It must be me."

The feelings that are kept inside and turned against oneself become what I call the INSO—the *internalized negative self-object*. As the child grows into an adult, those feelings are not outgrown. Even the angry rebellion of a teenager doesn't eradicate the real, internalized anger from childhood. Underneath the veneer of adult life, the INSO lives on, feeling deficient, angry, afraid, and ashamed. If you have an INSO, you most likely don't even know it. Just as I mentioned about the stories we tell ourselves, these feelings have become accepted, automatic, like looking both ways before crossing a busy street.

While you're growing up, no one talks about you having an INSO. Yet, because there are no absolutely perfect homes, you carry some form of INSO underneath your veneer. No one escapes, because everyone has, at some time in their young lives, been hurt. The INSO inside you could be based on anyone who ever abused you, degraded you, or treated you poorly in some other way. Typically, the INSO is based on someone who was dominant, such as a parent, teacher, sibling, bully, and so on.

Again, the INSO is internalized anger toward yourself that you took on as a child. As an adult, it shows itself in different ways as a coping strategy. One of those ways is as sexually compulsive behavior. And, just like crossing the street, the sexually compulsive behavior is automatic—until you identify its origin.

■ *Brett's INSO Has an Attitude*

A lot of people think Brett has an attitude. You probably know this kind of guy. He's quick to anger, easily offended, and almost always believes the other person is wronging him or disparaging him in some way. Any time someone says anything remotely disagreeable to Brett, his first response is anger. Why?

When Brett was a child, his parents seemingly hated each other and were probably staying together just for Brett and his brother. Both parents were angry much of the time. Under their anger was pain, which they avoided and denied. Brett's father was a former Marine who, beneath his macho exterior, felt insecure as a man. He tried to make up for this by being a bully with his children. If Brett or his brother didn't finish every single vegetable on their dinner plate, their father would scream at them. They were forced to sit at the dinner table, sometimes until two or three in the morning, until they finally ate what was left.

But, as a small child, Brett did not blame his father. Instead, he blamed himself. He felt ashamed that he couldn't eat everything and that he was disappointing his father. Brett was dependent on his father, and as Fairbairn and his colleagues showed in their research, rather than feeling his anger, Brett internalized it. In addition, Brett was able to pick up on the pain his parents felt, and he internalized those feelings as well.

As an adult, Brett still had the internalized pain and anger living inside him in the form of an INSO. Because Brett had never acknowledged it and didn't recognize it, he was at the mercy of his INSO. In a split second, it pushed him to react with irritation and even rage. What could Brett do about this? The first step was to become aware that he had an INSO. The second step was to engage in dialogue with it.

Brett: INSO, what's up?

INSO: I'm not talking.

Brett: Come on—cut the crap. I'm onto you. I know who you are.

INSO: Yeah? Who's that?

Brett: You're the feelings that have been trapped in me. The feelings of hurt, anger, fear, and shame. Feelings that I couldn't express 'cause I was too young. The crazy home I came from. I couldn't be angry at Dad or Mom. I didn't understand how out of balance our home life was. I couldn't blame them. So I blamed myself. That's who you are, INSO.

INSO: Get over it. That's just psychobabble—some bullshit that your therapist is feeding you. You're a fuck-up. Don't blame it on your parents.

Brett: No, I really get it. I know now why I've always felt schizophrenic. It's you! Now that I know about you, I can be aware. I can be in the now. I can stop living in reaction to my history, which includes you. I need you to cowboy up now. I need you to convert this crazy, negative thinking to positive, adult behaviors and thinking. Have you ever thought of that, INSO? You're not even real. You're just part of my story. I want you to be here with me now!

INSO: Seems too hard. I'm here to continue to torment you and keep you needing addiction to get relief. Let's forget this and go look at porn.

Brett: And I see you now. You're actually just smoke— just energy and some memories.

INSO: You sure are acting strong. Can I trust you?

Brett: For sure. It's safe now. And we have a lot to accomplish. With your help we can have peace, joy, serenity, abundance, and prosperity.

The fear of shame does not have a "face." It has a feeling, a sense, and a presence. It creates a separation from others. The internalized negative self-object, or INSO, does not have to be connected with the parents you internalized. The INSO can be connected to any experience you had in the past. When a traumatic event occurs in your life, the impact of the event does not miraculously vanish once the event is over.

As Peter Levine and Maggie Kline write in *Trauma Through a Child's Eyes*, trauma is in the nervous system, not in the event. Trauma situations—including the helplessness, terror, and shock they cause—remain in the nervous system, which impacts both your mind and body, feelings and thoughts—your emotional-mental database (Levine 2007). For example, if, as a child, you were bitten or even frightened by a snarling dog, you may have at least a little fear of dogs now. If you're walking on a sidewalk and a large dog is barking and straining on its leash, you feel a hesitancy inside yourself, a little pull of fear, or an urge to cross the street.

■ Chuck's Story: Secrets as a Trigger

Chuck grew up in a family where he was the scapegoat. His mother, his father, and especially an older brother, Sam, consistently gave him messages that he was worthless, and they used whatever he said to make fun of him. In response, Chuck learned to be as secretive as possible. When Chuck was a teenager, Sam dragged him to street prostitutes, which Chuck experienced as degrading. Eventually, Chuck developed an INSO that resembled his older brother, Sam.

As an adult, Chuck's sexually compulsive behavior took the form of masturbating to fantasies of being degraded. After marrying, Chuck had difficulty having sex with his wife. He kept being drawn to masturbate to degrading fantasies. After Chuck sought treatment, he was able to identify his internalized negative self-object based on his older brother. This "INSO Sam" would encourage Chuck to have sexually degrading fantasies and participate in online chat rooms where he could feel degraded.

Chuck was able to dialogue with INSO Sam and gradually transformed the need to feel degraded into a desire for positive love and affection in his relationship with his wife. However, because of his childhood coping strategy of keeping secrets from his family, he still had an INSO trigger around secrets. When Chuck's wife found out that he had gone to the movies one afternoon without telling her, she kidded him about keeping secrets. Instead of feeling in on the joke, Chuck reacted with shame.

The movie had been an action-adventure film and wasn't connected to Chuck's past sexually compulsive behavior. Yet feeling accused of keeping secrets was enough to send Chuck's INSO Sam into a tailspin, encouraging him to protect himself. Once INSO Sam again had a foothold in Chuck's life, it exerted its power to the extent that Chuck reverted to masturbating to degrading fantasies. Chuck needed to go back and once again dialogue with INSO Sam to minimize its influence in his life.

This example demonstrates two aspects of dealing with an INSO:

- *The addictive trigger that calls up your INSO does not necessarily have to be sexual in order to induce you to resort to sexually compulsive behavior.*

- *An INSO can be a powerful subpersonality and, even after you have lessened its impact, it may rise from the dead like a monster in a horror movie until you've converted that energy into something useful.*

By converting your INSO energy into positive thoughts and behaviors, you can take much of the life out of it. After that, it may always be part of you, but it won't have the same hold over your life.

EXERCISE: Finding Your INSO

How do you know if you have an INSO? How do you get in touch with an INSO? First, look for clues in behavior. Is a part of you causing you to hold back in your life? Do you fear certain triggering situations or actions? When an event occurs that triggers your fear, are you using addictive sexually compulsive behaviors to dull the pain? Second, try dialoging with an INSO to see if you get a response. Ask whatever questions occur to you. If no questions come to mind, take five minutes and ask the INSO the following questions:

- Are you there, INSO?

- Are you afraid or ashamed?

- What are you afraid or ashamed of?

- Can you remember any fearful or shameful event or situation that is still very strong for you?

- Did you blame yourself for what happened?

- Are you holding me back?

- Can we work together to no longer be in fear and shame, and no longer blame ourselves?

If you do "hear" from your INSO and have a dialogue, remember to tell your INSO that if there is a scared little child inside of you, that child is safe now. There is no more danger. The adult you will look after the scared child. You are on his side. He no longer needs to blame himself for what happened. He no longer needs to have the anger or fear or shame that he turned against himself. Keep reminding the child that you will keep him safe.

If your INSO is your internalized father, that's who you need to deal with. If it's your brother, that's who you need to dialogue with, and so on.

In the next chapter I'll describe Blue Sky and High Heels, which is another technique for catching your addictive impulses.

CHAPTER 9

Blue Sky and High Heels: *Understanding Your Addictive Triggers*

The chapter on the Blonde in the Beemer was about what to do when you lose yourself in a fantasy once it starts. The technique I call "Blue Sky and High Heels" is about being triggered by euphoric recall. As explained in chapter 3, euphoric recall is when a present-moment experience triggers the recall of a previous seemingly pleasurable experience. For example, when you eat pizza as an adult, it might recall the fun of eating with your family as a child. Another example could be seeing an older car of a particular make and model, which spurs you to remember your first sexual experience in the backseat of a similar car when you were in high school. Blue Sky and High Heels can be subtler than the Blonde in the Beemer. The trigger doesn't have to be sexual. It can be as simple and seemingly innocent as gazing at the blue sky.

Blue Sky and High Heels

About ten years ago, I was walking up the stairway to my second-floor counseling office when I heard a distinctive sound from the floor below. It sounded like high heels. I felt a strange, internal sensation as I continued up the steps. By the time I got to my floor, I realized I was suffering from the triggering of some historically sexual subpersonality within myself. Although such feelings were not particularly unusual, this moment on the stairs was quite powerful.

After walking into my office, I sat and gazed out the window at the beautiful blue California sky. In an instant, or what I like to call "quicker than clock time," I was transformed back into the sense of being the powerless sex addict that ruined most of my early life. Now, once again, I could fall back into helplessness over the intense desire to act out sexually. What really troubled me about this feeling was that I was having it right in my own counseling office, where I talked to other sex addicts every day.

Fortunately, I had access to the skills I had learned and developed during years of recovery and psychological training—the same techniques I am teaching you in this book. I gripped the arms of the chair and spoke aloud, repeating, "What is this really? What is this really?" My forehead perspired from my intense internal struggle. I kept breathing deeply and asking the same question, "What is this really?" while hanging onto the chair's armrests for dear life.

Demystifying the Power of a Trigger

After what seemed like hours (actually, about three minutes), a positive inner voice said, "Remember how you used to drive across the Bay Bridge to the O'Farrell Theatre in San Francisco? And how, while driving across the bridge, you'd look up at the blue sky and say to yourself, 'Please don't let me go here!' Then you would go to the theater anyway and 'hear' the high heels?" Many memories rushed back into my mind.

Next, as I sat in my office and sunk down into my essence, the association of blue skies and the high heels of the women performing at the adult theater began to dissolve. After using the technique of sinking into my essence, I could no longer react automatically to the trigger of the high heels and the blue skies. The process I went through is what I will explain further in this chapter. The challenge is to dislodge the energy from the offending subpersonality so that you can disrupt the memory trigger. I've never had another Blue Sky and High Heels experience since I demystified it. However, it's best to remember that you may have many different triggers. In fact, anything related to euphoric recall can be your version of Blue Sky and High Heels.

What I went through is similar to the patterns that happen to you every day. Just like me, you are preprogrammed about simple, everyday behaviors, such as what to buy, where to eat, and what to do next. We are all programmed by our history. Most of this programming is fine. Where the programming can exert more emphasis in your life is around sex. The triggers and the sexually compulsive behaviors and associations we have connected with them are what we sex addicts need to clear out. It's not unlike cleaning up the hard drive on your computer and installing new software.

Any combination of events can cause us to sexualize, and these key combinations stem from memory. I've seen blue sky thousands of times, but seeing it in tandem with the sound of high heels constituted a trigger. Suddenly, in my mind, I was on the Bay Bridge, driving to the O'Farrell Theatre. At first I found it terrifying, since I could encounter the combination of blue sky and high heels any time. But then I clearly saw that the answer wasn't forbidding myself to look at the blue sky anymore. It's just that I need to be aware that the combination of blue sky and high heels is a trigger for me.

Blue Sky and High Heels triggers can be sounds, sights, smells, tastes, or other sensations. You could be walking down the street in the midst of a cell phone conversation, barely paying attention to the area, and suddenly you hear music and catch the distinct smell of a bar. You think of a sexual encounter that started in a bar and, suddenly, you're triggered. You feel that you *need* to act out sexually. It can happen any time, and you can be prepared by becoming aware of your triggers so that you're no longer reacting automatically.

You Don't Have to Pull the Trigger

What does it mean to be triggered? It means your addict is pulling the trigger on the gun he's holding to your head to pressure you into doing something really stupid. By this point in the book, you may be able to push the gun away so it's no longer in your face (especially if you've tried some of the techniques I've suggested, such as dialoging with your addict). You may be able to shake your head and say, "Not now, Buddy. You're not going to mug me this time." But what about the next time? And the next?

What will you do the next time you get an "uncontrollable" impulse? What if you could practice what to do when you're triggered sexually, but with a trigger that has less power over you? For example, you can notice which foods trigger positive or negative feelings, what triggers you to get ticked off at someone you work with, or which drivers trigger you when you're in heavy traffic. You can notice the events that get to you, especially situations that lead you to excessive behaviors or things that trigger you to react aggressively. You can hunt down these situations and, rather than reacting automatically, you can become aware of your patterns and maybe even smile to yourself when you see the triggers. You can reach a turning point where you no longer react negatively to triggering situations.

You can begin by noticing a few innocent triggers, such as seeing a fast food ad on TV and feeling the urge to jump in your car and get a big, greasy burger. This is a way to begin to notice the cues in your mind and your body that alert you to an impulse. In this example, you might say to yourself, "No. I don't need to go anywhere right now. I just want to finish watching the game. Instead, I'll grab that bag of chips on the counter." If you can do this with food impulses, for example, you can begin to become aware of the process by which you note and counteract the urge to act in a negative way. Then you can learn to apply this process to your sexually compulsive behavior patterns.

The first step is to notice the situations that tend to trigger you. The second step is to demystify the sensations of inappropriate desire so that, rather than giving in to the urges, you stay in touch with yourself and your essence. An example is how seeing blue sky and hearing the sound of high heels triggered me and I demystified it by remembering that it was associated with driving to an adult theater. Say no, and feel what happens inside you then. Usually there will be some push-back, some resistance to your refusal to give in. This feeling is known as *withdrawal* in addiction circles. Yet you can weather this resistance. You *can* challenge your automatic responses, the programming generated by your internal story.

The third step is to demonstrate to yourself that you can, indeed, resist what has been triggering you to act out in sexually compulsive ways. You can very consciously show yourself that you no longer need to be a slave to your impulses. I've had clients who have walked into what used to be their favorite sexual massage parlor, courteously told the woman at the front desk that they wouldn't be coming back, and then left, feeling extremely self-empowered. This is a great way to prove to yourself that you're serious about recovery. But if you decide to take this route, be sure to be polite and always stay within the law.

I've also had a number of clients who have trouble with Internet porn. They know that they'll soon be going to their computers to check e-mail, and then it will be so easy to wander over to a familiar porn site. I advise these clients to set a limit for themselves and step away from the computer when they feel the impulse to hit the porn site. I've found that when these clients are able to hold to these limits, they not only feel good—they feel heroic. They have triumphed over their sexually addictive behavior. They should feel great. It's hard to stay focused when at the computer. To help, I tell my clients to watch their mind and, if need be, to change it.

■ *Larry: Startled at Starbucks*

There are times when a trigger can echo, or continue on for days or weeks, but in a less powerful form. Taking a break from work, Larry stopped by his local Starbucks for coffee and a donut. After he made the purchase, he sat down at one of the small, round tables. He glanced up as a strikingly beautiful woman walked in the door and brushed past his table on her way to the counter. At first, he only said to himself, "What a gorgeous woman!" As Larry lifted his coffee for another sip, he noticed that the woman had moved to the counter and had her back to him. She was wearing a varsity-type jacket with these words on the back: "Bite Me."

Suddenly, Larry's mind seemed to fall apart completely. Although he wasn't even sure what "Bite Me" meant on the woman's jacket, he suddenly imagined himself performing oral sex on the woman. It was just for a millisecond, but that was long enough for the familiar radical chemical shift to occur in Larry's metabolism. If you are a sex addict, you most likely know what I mean by this feeling in your body. Larry became so disoriented that he momentarily forgot he was drinking coffee. But Larry's experience didn't end there.

Just driving by that Starbucks on another day, he again had a sexual-chemical shift in his body. It was smaller than when he first saw the woman in the Starbucks, but he still felt compelled to look through the Starbucks window to see if the woman happened to be inside. Just as the blue sky triggered me, for months Larry was triggered by every single Starbucks he saw.

Fortunately, Larry was able to dialogue with his addict and not act out sexually. But it was an important lesson in the power of an event to become associated with a geographical location or locations. If this happens to you, notice what has triggered these feelings and take steps to desensitize yourself to the trigger. One way to do this is just by noticing what you're going through. The associations can even become amusing. I'll offer an example of this later in the chapter.

■ Darnell's Blue Sky Dialogue

Before he began to change his sexually compulsive behavior, Darnell had a pattern of going to his computer to check the latest sports scores. He told himself that he was only going to the computer to check on sports, which was just fine. But after checking a few sites for sports scores and news, he always seemed to wander over to a porn site. He convinced himself that it would be just for a few moments, but after he hit the site, he was triggered enough to stay on it hours longer *than he had planned. Once triggered, it was almost as if there was no turning back.*

Darnell began to explore his history and was eventually able to see that his search for sports scores was the first step in his trigger. As he became more aware, he was able to begin to change his behavior. One step in changing was to dialogue with his addict, whom Darnell called Pornell:

Darnell: We're just going to sip our coffee and check out what players got traded this week.

Pornell: No way! You know that once we're at the computer, we have to look at our favorite "cream pie" adult site.

Darnell: Not this time. I know that sitting at the computer to check out sports is my Blue Sky and High Heels. So, before we walked in here to sit at the computer, I prepared myself.

Pornell: Oh, you're prepared all right. You're prepared to drop your pants and rub one out.

Darnell: Not going to happen. As soon as I walked into this room, before I even sat down at the computer, I knew I would have thoughts about going to a porn site.

Pornell: Of course—because that's what we want to do. That's what we're here for.

Darnell: That's not what we're here for. That only leads to feeling bad later. We're here to check sports and check e-mail. So, before I even sit at the computer, I say to myself "sports and e-mail, sports and e-mail."

Pornell: That's stupid.

Darnell: No. What you want to do, jacking off to porn, that's what's stupid. Staying with sports and e-mail is me playing it smart.

Because Darnell knew ahead of time that just going to the computer was his Blue Sky and High Heels trigger, he could prepare himself. He knew that Pornell was going to start jabbering in his mind. But Darnell also knew that he no longer had to listen to what Pornell wanted. He could stay focused on "sports and e-mail" rather than giving in to Pornell's focus. Each time Darnell successfully went to the computer without opening a porn site, he felt more and more successful.

By knowing ahead of time that a situation can prompt your Blue Sky and High Heels moment, you can be prepared. Darnell could have stopped ever using a computer, but that, of course, was not practical. What is practical is to be prepared and make a different choice.

■ *Rand's Blue Sky and High Heels*

Similar to using a computer, there are many Blue Sky and High Heels moments that cannot avoided. Rand's happened every time he started the water running to take a shower. In fact, it kicked in the moment he got his towel and washcloth ready. At that moment, he knew he was going to start his fantasy story running and end up masturbating in the shower, rather than seeking intimacy with his wife in the next room.

For Rand, a step toward breaking the stranglehold of his sexually compulsive behavior was seeking out other instances in which he was triggered in a way that was powerful, though not sexual. For example, every time Rand packed up his car with baseball equipment, he began mentally preparing himself to play on the field. He noticed how his adrenaline would start pumping. As Rand said, "When I finally stepped onto the field, I was ready for battle. "

It was much easier for Rand to notice his behavior and the chemical shift in his body when he was getting ready to play baseball than it was for him to become aware that his addict was going to be triggered to engage in sexually compulsive behavior. But by noticing the shift that occurred when he was preparing to walk out onto the baseball diamond, he began to become more aware how his body reacted to triggers. He began to spot the signs that he was gearing up in response to an urge. He would notice as he began to shift to a higher state of excitement. This growing awareness of his body's signals and the thoughts that triggered them helped him when he was getting ready to shower. As his mind kicked in and prepared to play his masturbation fantasy, Rand was gradually able to note the changes and fight back against his sexually compulsive behavior. As I've mentioned many times in this book, there is nothing wrong with sex or masturbation. What we are seeking is freedom from sexually compulsive behavior that leads to feelings of shame and defeat.

That Magic-Fingers Feeling

Notice when your attention locks in on sexualizing or objectifying. You may be triggered. Watch for the sexual charge. Be fascinated by it. You don't have to act on it. Being sexually charged doesn't mean you have to have an orgasm. Many of the men I've spoken to in counseling felt like they had to have an orgasm within an hour of having a Blue Sky and High Heels experience. It doesn't have to be that way. Getting triggered and needing to have an orgasm is a pattern that is going to screw up your day, your relationships, and your mind.

The difficult part is that this is so automatic and subtle that you might not even notice when you're triggered. So work on noticing when you get that charge. When you can get between the impulse and the action, you can change the outcome. It's as if someone said, "Would you like me to punch you in the mouth?" Your addict is basically saying the same thing by pushing you to engage in behavior that will have negative consequences for your life. But you don't have to get punched in the mouth—or the balls, as it were.

One technique you can use is to create a cue for yourself. A *cue* is a word or action you can use to signal or alert yourself to wake up to what's happening in the moment. The Beard Test I described in chapter 4 is a signal or cue I use to remember that I'm a man, rather than a weakling at the mercy of my addict.

Two words that I use as a cue are "Magic Fingers." For me, Magic Fingers is the energy strumming on my chest. The energy runs through my solar plexus. Then I start to feel it moving toward my genitals. If you have a word for the energy you feel when you first begin to get sexually aroused or triggered in a situation that is not appropriate, you can practice saying those words to yourself.

You will first need to notice the feeling in your chest or your genitals. If you can notice that, you can ask yourself, "Is this appropriate?" You may not catch the sensations the first time. Instead, you'll act out. The third time maybe you'll wait to act out. By the fourth time, you might find yourself saying, "This is crazy. I've got work to do." Your mind will start to change. The point is to distract yourself from the chemical release, or your addictive thinking, and convert that energy into something positive.

What I call the Magic Fingers response is actually your mind working on you to create a chemical release. This energy runs through your body and to your genitals, gearing you up for sexual release. When you sense this energy surge, you have an opportunity to be your own hero. You can say to yourself, "This is not the right time. This is not the right place. This is not the right person. I've got work to do. I've got a relationship to be in. I'm not going to objectify that woman across the restaurant and think about her later while I'm having sex with my wife."

Watch for Blue Sky and High Heels experiences that can be triggered while being out with the guys. You may consider them your friends, but watch how they talk about women. Notice if you start getting that Magic Fingers feeling. I no longer have friends who talk about going to strip clubs or massage parlors. Instead, I have friends who talk about race cars, psychology, and football. I also have a wonderfully trusting and intimate relationship with my wife.

The Centerfold Versus Reality

No one taught me what was normal. Everyone taught me that pussy was like gold or a million-dollar bill. Each woman had this million-dollar bill between her legs, and my whole objective was to get it. Another way of saying this is that my objectification of a woman fueled my objective to get between her legs. This objectification of women is personified by the perfect-looking centerfold. As I matured as a person and as a man, I realized that each woman is a whole person, not just a hole. I began to experience the entire person, and a whole, real person has various behaviors, moods, thoughts, ideas, opinions, feelings, and bodily functions.

For most addicts who act out sexually, the fantasy is not about a real woman who talks and has smells and has bodily functions. It couldn't be. Fantasies are not real. Porn is not real. The women photographed in porn magazines and who appear on porn sites or in porn videos are not being real. Consequently, one effective technique for breaking the stranglehold of sexually addictive triggers is to imagine the woman as a real person—which, of course, she is. We looked at this briefly in chapter 6, but it's worth going into in more depth here. For example, when you find yourself objectifying or sexualizing a woman, visualize her sitting on the toilet moving her bowels. (Of course, don't imagine anything that arouses you.) Or she has some physical feature that you find unattractive, and this attribute is revealed when she's naked. Maybe her armpits smell. Or you can imagine that she passes gas almost continuously—and loudly—and she has skid marks on her panties. Now, I understand that this isn't very pretty. But when you visualize that the woman has bodily functions, it is more difficult to objectify or sexualize her. What you're doing is interfering with the addict's fantasy to loosen the hold that the fantasy has over you. You are making a choice.

EXERCISE: Notice Your Triggers

This exercise is designed to give you concrete steps to take so that you can notice when you are triggered and then disrupt the triggering process.

1. Notice how your senses are constantly monitoring your environment. You are actually thinking unconsciously to keep yourself protected. Although that sounds contradictory, it means that you are both consciously and unconsciously aware of what is happening around you.

2. Create a cue to alert yourself to what's happening in the moment. You could use something like the Beard Test, or pick one or two words you say to yourself, such as "Magic Fingers." This can help bring you back to conscious reality and break the flow of the fantasy.

3. Notice when you feel a body sensation or your focus locks on a woman.

4. Become aware of your Blue Sky and High Heels—your own, unique triggers.

5. Notice if you feel a Magic Fingers type of change in your body.

6. Say your cue to yourself and stop the Magic Fingers sensation from escalating to the point where you need to act out.

7. Practice this for at least five minutes a day for two days or more. Start to notice that the Blue Sky and High Heels triggers are really coping strategies—figments of your addictive imagination.

8. When you can confront your addictive behavior triggers and make a choice not to give in to your addict, feel the incredible success in that.

In the next chapter we'll further explore the reality that you always have a choice and the techniques you can use to make positive choices.

CHAPTER 10

You Always Have a Choice

A man called my office from his home in Canada. From his slurred speech, it was obvious he had had one beer too many, and he spoke in a way that indicated he was feeling sorry for himself. His wife had gone away for a few days, and his addict subpersonality wanted to go on a masturbation binge. I told him he had a choice. He could meet the addict's demand with a coping strategy, such as medicating (in his case, drinking) to stop feeling alone or lonely. Alternatively, he could dialogue with his addict and do something else—anything but the addictive behavior. He did have a choice.

This is what I want you to remember: No matter how strong the pull toward sexually compulsive behavior, you always have a choice. Even though your mind tells you to drink, look at porn, have sex, masturbate, see a prostitute, visit a strip club, or just walk around the mall to look at women, you always have a choice. It's your birthright to have a choice. You don't have to give in to the addict within. You can choose something else to do. You can say, "What else?"

Whether you give in to your addict or not, this is your real life and there are real consequences. It's your marriage. Your kids. Your job. Your finances. Your peace of mind. In chapter 9, I explained Blue Sky and High Heels and what to do when you get triggered. Some men seek out situations where they know they'll be triggered. Maybe you do, too. Just remember: you always have a choice.

■ *Jonathan's Nude Beach Choice*

In the course of his work as a buyer for a major U.S. wine-importing company, Jonathan frequently traveled to Europe. For exercise, Jonathan ran about nine miles a day. If he was in a city on the coast of France, he could have chosen to jog past the rustic old churches or the vineyards at the outskirts of the city. Instead, Jonathan usually chose to run toward his version of Blue Sky and High Heels—the beaches where many women sunbathed topless. He was, of course, triggered and would act out sexually by seeking a prostitute or returning to his hotel to masturbate. But once the episode was over, Jonathan felt shame and sank into feelings of depression over how weak he was—until the next time he went out for a run.

Through our counseling work together, Jonathan began to dialogue with his addict. He did this even while he was in the middle of a run. He needed to keep reminding himself that he always had a choice. He gradually took charge so that he was consciously choosing which route he took while jogging. When he "slipped" and suddenly found himself running by a topless beach, he would practice saying a trigger-breaking word to himself. In Jonathan's case, the word was "shame." If he didn't veer away from the topless beach, he would end up feeling a deep sense of shame. When he did turn away, he felt success.

If you know what places and situations trigger you, you can choose to avoid those locations or settings. Being "weak" or lacking self-control is just giving in to your addict. I have had clients who go to the mall just so they can skulk by Victoria's Secret and furtively glance inside. They were hoping to possibly catch sight of a woman picking up a bra or walking into a dressing room. That visual was enough to trigger a fantasy. Yet, from the moment they decided to turn toward the mall, to getting out of the parked car, to the first glance inside the store, each of these men had a choice to make: to give in to their addict or to refuse.

When you find yourself giving in, you can dialogue with your addict and seek an agreement to avoid places and situations that will trigger you to act out sexually. As I've mentioned before, you can dialogue in your mind, but it is much more effective to do this in writing. In addition, as you learned in chapter 9, you can set up a cue or code word that you can say to yourself to counter the trigger. Some of my clients use silly or goofy words to lighten up the situation and short-circuit the addiction into humor And you can always remind yourself that you have a choice by saying, "What else?" "What else can I do now?" If you work on this practice, the pull to act out will become less and less compelling.

Choice throughout Your Life

The truth is that you have always had a choice. But as you grew up and were influenced and conditioned by your family and your life situations, your choices became more limited. Because you thought you were too short or too tall, because a girl turned you down for a date, or whatever happened to you, you started creating a story for yourself.

As your story about who you were became more entrenched, your choices about everything diminished. Because of your story, your choice about whether to ask out the cheerleader (or whatever the situation was in your case) was practically nonexistent. Even if you didn't notice, your options diminished and you narrowed your behaviors and beliefs to fit into the unique story you'd created. You began to believe that you had fewer choices than you actually did.

When you increase your conscious awareness and wake up to who you really are (as opposed to what your story says you are), you can be anything within your limitations. For example, I'm not going to be a pro baseball player. But I can and did stop living a life in which I was overwhelmed by sexually compulsive behaviors. As you stop living according to the limitations of the story that had you believing you were helpless or had you ashamed or in fear, you can make different choices. When your story changes, you can begin to replace acting out with true intimacy with a real person, if that is what you choose to do.

Changing your story doesn't mean that you'll stop admiring the female body. The intent of this book is not to neuter you. What I want is for you to experience your choice to be free of sexually compulsive thoughts and behaviors. You may always love the sight of a naked woman. Yet, when you choose to move away from addiction, the woman no longer has to be an object. She becomes a real person, with thoughts, feelings, smells, and other attributes. She is a person to be appreciated and admired.

When I was caught in the web of sexually compulsive behavior, I would get triggered by seeing a beautiful woman at a store or coffee shop. I would obsess about her all day until I could get to a video store. There, I would spend at least half an hour trying to find a porn video with an actress who looked like the woman I had seen. Many of my counseling clients have done the same behavior or something similar. Leaving the video store, I would spend more fruitless time watching the porn and repeatedly masturbating, pretending the woman on the video was the woman I had seen earlier in the day. I felt ashamed and embarrassed. I felt weak. I was stuck in a loop of addictive negative thinking, stuck in my negative story about myself.

The next day I would do exactly the same thing when I was triggered by the sight of an attractive woman in the grocery store, the post office, or wherever. At that time, I hadn't realized that I had a choice. I felt compelled. But I did have a choice and, as I progressed in my recovery, I began making different, more positive choices. These included the option to ask myself, "What else?"

Always Remember: What Else?

Working with the techniques you've learned in preceding chapters, you've begun to experience the truth that you're not your story. You probably also know too much to keep pretending that you need to go along with the sexually compulsive pull of your addict. This pull is created by your mind, which works incredibly quickly, in a seemingly automatic way. Your mind works on you to get you to believe you have no choice. But you do. You can say no or "What else?"

My favorite thing to say is, "What else?" What do you want to do besides act out sexually? Practice saying it. Keep using the lessons you've already learned and incorporate saying, "What else?" If you've been observing your thoughts and dialoguing with your subpersonalities, you have the skill to separate positive thoughts from the negative and damaging ones. Now it's time to learn to see those negative and damaging thoughts galloping toward you and head them off at the pass. You don't have to live your life on automatic. You can let go of living in reaction to your history.

When you practice noticing what your mind is doing and not going along with it, it's like installing new "addiction detection" software that intercepts the old, addictive impulses. It takes practice, and it may not be so easy at first. But keep at it. If you get frustrated and give up, you are giving in to your addict. If you practice and use the tools I describe in this and earlier chapters, your mind will change. You will start making better choices and, eventually, you won't have as many addictive impulses to defend against. Those that do arise will be like fruit flies buzzing around your head. Using the tools that you've learned here, you can begin to easily shoo them away.

Conversation with Choice Point

Remember, it's your birthright to have a choice. What I'd like you to do next is to learn to notice the exact point where you can make a choice. This point may be when your addict is pulling you toward the computer to look at porn and you give in, "just this one last time." Or it could be when you notice a woman on the street, don't look away, and start to spin a sexual fantasy about her. When you give in to your addict, you're making a choice. The moment you make that choice is what I call the *choice point*. That moment is also when you can make a different choice. Consider Barry's dialogue with his addict. Barry thinks of his ability to choose as "software" he's installed in his brain. Let's see how the dialogue plays out.

Barry: You seem to be restless. Just because your wife went shopping doesn't mean that you get to beat off to porn.

Addict: Screw you! I haven't beat off in two months! Why not?

Barry: Because I'm paying attention to the choice point. I get to choose now, and I'm choosing to have sex later with my wife rather than doing the porn thing today.

Addict: Screw that. Too much trouble. What if she doesn't want to? Come on! We have the time and opportunity now!

Barry: Come on yourself. Just getting off isn't where we're at anymore. Remember? What else do you want to do?

Addict: Shit! You're so strict! Why can't I con you anymore?

Barry: Because I've installed Choice Point. Before, I didn't know I could choose. You and I just lived like our history told us to and I kept jerking off to porn. Now I know better, and I choose to say no. It's actually more fun to be with a real, live person I love. Wow! I said it. I can love now. I can have healthy sex without guilt or shame.

Your Story, Your Choice, Your Life

If you're stuck in your story of not having a choice, you will continue to want to do the same thing over and over and wish that it was better. You may drink the same drinks. You may keep the same friends. You might not stop masturbating to porn. Mind seems to resist change, even for the better. One way to work on changing your mind is to think of what else you'd like to do, and maybe even come up with a list of things you've always wanted to do. Maybe you wanted to change your life in some dynamic way.

Most of the people who come to me do change their minds, and sometimes they also change their careers. I had a client who said, "I saw my dad being a postman, so I became a postman too. I actually wanted to be a veterinarian." This client began to make positive choices in his life, he stopped acting out sexually, and his self-esteem increased. He made a choice to see if, even though he was older now, he could become a veterinarian. Although it was difficult going back to school, he did it. His reward was doing what he loves—working with animals. I have had clients who were Silicon Valley millionaires. They made new choices to begin doing what they really loved, such as teaching high school.

Here is what one client told his addict subpersonality about the choice point. This realization was pivotal in his recovery:

"What difference would it make if I could have gotten laid twenty times a week. All that would have gotten me is divorced. Your whole plan is nothing but a plan for disaster! What I'm telling you is that I want to assume full responsibility for everything that I've done. I'm the one who has to live with the pain. I was the one who felt like crap last week. I do not blame anybody. I know that I have a choice. I can choose to go and jack off in front of the computer, and I can choose to live my sad story over and over. I can also choose to create a new and better story. I can start to see myself as I truly am. I can tell the story of my life—the real story of how I've succeeded and how I have overcome adversity and rejection."

My Story of Making a Choice

In my own recovery, I also worked on remembering that I always had a choice. One day, I was dialoging with my addict subpersonality. At that time, I was in graduate school and was learning to ask myself, "What else?" It was early in my recovery, and one day I asked my addict what else it wanted to do besides acting out sexually. Addict replied: "Fuck you." I kept asking for days, and Addict kept replying with the same two-word phrase. Finally, Choice Point—the part of myself that could see that I had a choice—spoke up and said, "A fireman."

Of course I knew I wasn't going to be a fireman. There was just a little boy inside me wanting to be a fireman. But I went to a fire station and asked to volunteer. They put a broom and dust mop in my hand and had me sweep, dust, and wax the fire trucks. I had a good time. After doing that for two months, I got to go out on a few fire calls, which was exciting and interesting.

But then was there a time when I asked Choice Point, "Do you like being a fireman?" Choice Point said, "No. I don't like the hours. I don't like the food. And they have those magazines we shouldn't be reading." Since I was in recovery, it was not a good idea for me to be around the adult magazines that some of the firemen in that fire station read. The next day I thanked the firemen and said I no longer needed to work there.

I had explored being a fireman, which I knew beforehand was an exercise. Now I asked Choice Point, "What else do you want to do?" Choice Point replied, "A race car driver." That's when I had a little red Honda modified for racing and later raced it at Laguna Seca Raceway, Thunderhill Raceway Park, and Infineon Raceway. Although I was not going to be a professional driver, tearing around these tracks was great fun, and a terrific What Else?

The point of my relating the fireman story is that I listened to Choice Point and tried something new. I tried a What Else? I followed my instinct rather than repeating what my old story said to do. It led me away from the old story *that was holding me back, keeping me separate, and keeping me from my true purpose in life. It led me more toward recovery and closer to being an addictions counselor and teacher.*

Each of us has an actual purpose. That includes you. It's okay to work at the post office or deliver mail. We need fine men and women who collect the trash and fix the roads. That's very important. But, whether you're collecting trash or running a big company, if you're not happy doing what you're doing, it's an ongoing train wreck. It can lead to drinking and taking drugs. It can bring misery to you and others. It can lead to sexually compulsive behavior. It can lead you to keep doing self-destructive behavior that is a coping mechanism to make you try and feel a little better, even if it's masturbating in a dark room to porn.

EXERCISE: You Always Have a Choice

The time to make a choice to stop acting out sexually is not when you're in the grips of it. At that moment, it's nearly impossible to change anything. The chemicals have already been released and your body is starting to react. The time to make a choice is when, as described in the preceding chapters about noticing triggers, you feel the shift toward sexually compulsive behavior starting. This exercise is designed to bring your choice point into focus. When you know what is useful and what is not useful, you can more easily make a clear choice and ask yourself: What else? What else can I do?

Take about ten minutes to do the following exercise:

1. Think about the ways in which you act out sexually when you give in to impulses.

2. Write down ten things that do damage to you when you act out sexually, such as at your job or in your relationships. You should write these down before your mind starts going and you get an erection.

3. Now write down ten things that would be useful for you to do.

4. Start thinking about what you really like, what you've always liked. Maybe it's basketball. You're not going to be a pro, but how could you be involved with it? If you like fly fishing, how can you get into it? Is it a hobby you can pursue? Google whatever interests you.

5. Start looking at what you love to do. According to a book called *Do What You Love, The Money Will Follow: Discovering Your Right Livelihood*, if you take steps toward living your dream, your finances will begin to coalesce around that dream (Sinetar 1989). Although that might be an oversimplification, there is a definite, tangible reward in doing what provides you joy rather than the fear, shame, and pain that result from addiction.

6. If you feel that first impulse to act out, ask yourself: What else? What else do you want to do besides being an addict, besides having a miserable life? What else do you want to do? What else?

Chapter 11 introduces you to your "Red Light Guy," a technique for changing negative sexual energy into positive behavior.

CHAPTER 11

Your Red Light Guy:
Change Sexual Energy into Positive Behavior

A few years ago, while driving to work, I came to the last traffic light just before my office. It was red, so I stopped. As I sat and waited for the green, I suddenly realized that I hadn't actually thought, *Here is a red light. I need to take my foot off the gas, put it on the brake, and stop.* I just automatically stopped the car. How amazing! I continued driving toward my office but continued to think about this phenomenon. I posited that there must be a part of me, inside my thinking processes, that looked out for me. This part of my mind had my foot step on the brake without me even having to consciously think about it.

I Meet My Red Light Guy

After I got to my office, I sat down and decided to mull this over. I considered how I had this amazing ability to do the general things that needed doing and to do them automatically. Was I a superhero? No. Every one of us does action after action automatically all day long. Did you think about brushing your teeth this morning? Did you think for a long time about tying your shoes?

Next, I thought, *What if I were to be able to harness this ability and use it to stop objectifying women on the street? What if that force within me could intercept whatever was left of my tendency to automatically objectify and sexualize—The Looker—and do this at any time and in any place?*

Just for fun, I called this internal force the "Red Light Guy," and I developed another way to interrupt or stop automatic responses: the Red Light Guy technique. I call it that because it is about automatic behavior, such as stopping at a red light. My Red Light Guy is the part of me that performs behaviors automatically and, at that point in my recovery, I wanted to stop automatically looking at women. You have your own version of the Red Light Guy. Once you become aware and communicate with him, you can make it so that your sexually compulsive behavior is no longer automatic. Although it may sound a little contradictory, finding your own Red Light Guy can enable you to both notice your automatic behavior and stop it.

Next, I decided that every time I noticed I was sexually triggered, such as when I looked at an attractive woman and was about to start a fantasy, I would put my hand on my heart and think to myself, *I'd like to shift this energy to some positive thought or behavior.* In terms of psychology, this is called "cognitive behavioral" thinking. *Cognitive behavioral therapy* emphasizes the role that thoughts play in creating and maintaining anxiety, anger, and behaviors. In other words, if you think positively about something, you will probably behave differently (Ronen and Freeman 2006).

Putting the Red Light Guy into Practice

To start using the Red Light Guy technique, I developed three basic steps: First, I noticed my behavior, which stopped me from being on automatic. Second, when I caught myself starting to look at a woman in a sexual way, I put my hand on my heart. Third, I thought to myself, "I'd like to shift this energy to some positive thought or behavior."

For the next two months, I tried out this technique. When my eyes wandered toward a woman who I knew would trigger me into my addiction (according to my addict's "radar"—automatically scanning for women), I would earnestly put my hand on my heart and tell myself that her body was none of my business. Gradually, it started to sink in that it really was not my business. As I did that, I noticed that I was starting to relax more in public. I had more energy for positive thoughts and feelings because there was less guilt and shame going on inside me.

I even realized that my addict's "radar" for objectifying women was starting to fade out. As its power faded, instead of drifting off into fantasies that were never going to happen, I began to notice other things, such as store windows with merchandise on display. How amazing! I noticed other people, couples holding hands, and happy families. I was no longer just on the lookout for attractive women to sexualize. Inside, I felt calmer. Life made more sense. That weird, electric, amped-up feeling I had been at the mercy of for so long was, thankfully, gone. I was more focused on what was happening in the moment.

It was also great to lose what I thought of as my "X-ray vision." You probably know what I mean. It's the absurd belief that I could actually "see" what was under women's clothing! Again, this was a crazy fantasy and, without it, life was easier. And it kept getting easier as I practiced this technique of putting my hand on my heart, making affirmations, and not objectifying women.

The first time I knew for certain this hand-on-heart technique was working occurred while I was in an upscale market searching for protein powder. I was walking down an aisle when I felt strongly compelled to look down and to the right. It was an instantaneous, huge, "radar" pull, with my addict yelling at me to "Look down! Right now! Now! Now!"

But instead of automatically looking, I continued to reach for the protein powder. I picked it up and, as I turned to continue down the aisle, I saw what my addict had been pleading with me to see: the beautiful woman who had been bending down to pick up a can of soup from a bottom shelf. She had on a low-cut blouse and no bra. It was what I used to think of as the "shot of a lifetime." But I only witnessed the last part, when she was almost standing. So I did not stare down her blouse. I just stopped in my tracks and thought to myself, *It works!*

A year before, I would've been angry that I missed an opportunity to catch sight of what would've got me going into my addictive response. The sight of the woman's exposed cleavage would have launched me into a full day of fantasy, a trip to the video store, a brief orgasm, and a night of shame. But that day, I was thrilled to experience that her body was none of my business. The Red Light Guy I had installed was working!

Then I had one of those you-had-to-be-there experiences. With my hand on my heart, I said out loud, "Thank you." I heard a voice next to me, looked up, and saw another attractive woman. She smiled, looked directly at me, and said, "You're welcome."

Of course, neither woman had known the inner process I had just gone through. But I don't want to believe that it was a coincidence. I'll always believe that the woman's words were meant just for me and were, in a sense, a reward for resisting sexually compulsive behavior.

As I walked toward the cash registers, a few tears came to my eyes. This episode may not seem like much, but it was a wonderful lesson for me. I had proven to myself that I was no longer at the mercy of my addict. I had the Red Light Guy technique to stop the addict's acting-out behavior, maybe even before it got started.

What You Can Do Now

As you continue to read this chapter, think about installing your Red Light Guy. You can call "him" that or something else. You can put your hand on your heart, like I do, or choose another action. The point is to take action. It's a step toward letting go of your "Looker"—which is the part of you that objectifies and sexualizes others.

You could call your version of the Red Light Guy the "Looker Stopper," or the "I'm Not Going There Again Guy." What matters is that you begin to notice when you look, when you objectify, and when you start spinning a fantasy that's going to lead to acting out. That's when you need your version of the Red Light Guy. That's when you need to stop. Take a minute, right now, and ask yourself to pay attention, to notice, and to take a step toward transforming the Looker energy into positive thoughts and actions.

I've worked with men who, once they installed a Red Light Guy and stopped their time-wasting behaviors, took steps toward changing jobs, starting new businesses, and finding more time to enjoy hobbies such as sailing or golf. Now, I'm not guaranteeing that this will happen to you. I am implying that you will feel better about yourself and your life will improve. It's definitely possible to shift from objectification of women to admiration.

You may be unaware that you have a guidance system pre-installed. It's an unconscious aspect of yourself that is running your life. Again, you are living in reaction to your history. Most of this is fine. You stop for red lights. You eat three times a day. You go to work in the morning. You pretty much do what you're supposed to do. That's the Red Light Guy. You couldn't function if you were constantly thinking, "I better stop for that red light. I need to tie my shoe. I need to put my pants on." So you do these things automatically. In the same way, you are on automatic around your sexuality. Installing a Red Light Guy can take you off automatic so that you are, instead, making conscious decisions. After a time, you may be surprised that your automatic behavior has changed so that you automatically *don't* objectify.

■ *Evan's Red Light Guy*

Evan worked in an office, and when the day was warm, he liked to spend his lunchtime outside. He especially enjoyed going to a burrito place where he would invariably look at the women in shorts and halter tops. Since he considered them already half naked, it was easy for him to imagine them completely nude. In fact, Evan believed so strongly in his X-ray vision that he actually thought his imaginary vision of what they looked like naked was accurate.

Evan had seen so many porn movies that his addict-self (whom he called his "Porn Guy") would project images of naked bodies onto any attractive woman he happened to spot. Because he had thousands of imprints of women's bodies in his mind, Evan would clearly visualize a woman's naked body and get turned on. Once he was back at his office, he would sneak into the men's room and masturbate.

Because Evan did this behavior almost every day, his wife would wonder why he didn't want to have sex very often. The truth was that Evan's wife, though attractive, did not look like a naked porn star—which is how Evan imagined the women he saw at the burrito place. Evan's wife was a regular human being (which was also true of the women at the burrito place, though not in Evan's mind). In Evan's mind, women were objectified to the point where the only thing that would be useful to him (or so his addict subpersonality believed) was the perfect woman. Of course, the women in the porn videos appeared perfect to Evan, though in real life they were women like any other woman, with smells and moods, likes and dislikes.

After a coworker almost caught Evan masturbating in the men's room, and after Evan's wife began to talk about a trial separation, Evan knew he had a decision to make. In counseling, one of the techniques that Evan employed was to install the Red Light Guy. Evan thought of it as installing new software in his mind. This new software would alert him when he was objectifying and have him perform a new action instead. Evan chose to touch his hand to his chest and say to himself, "Real woman."

The first few times Evan went back to the burrito place and saw an attractive young woman, he automatically began to sexualize, imagining her as a naked porn star. Then Evan began to catch himself as he started to stare. The Red Light Guy would activate, and Evan would touch his hand to his chest, saying quietly, "Real woman." Evan would look away and take a deep breath. For Evan, "real woman" meant not only that the woman he saw was a real woman, but also that he wanted to be in a relationship with one specific real woman—his wife.

It wasn't easy for Evan to change his behavior, which meant changing his mind. For years, he had watched porn movies and had automatically sexualized and objectified thousands of women. But the stakes for Evan were high enough that he forced himself to practice activating the Red Light Guy, touching his chest and saying the words "real woman" to himself.

Similar to the experience I had when I installed a Red Light Guy, after a few months Evan began to feel more relaxed. Instead of Porn Guy running Evan's life, the Red Light Guy was there watching out for him every moment of the day. Evan no longer had to objectify and then act out through masturbating in the men's room at work. At home, he smiled more and was available to make love with his wife. Again, it wasn't easy for Evan to change his behavior. It took practice and vigilance. The reward for Evan was no longer feeling at the mercy of his impulses. Although it took many more months, Evan gradually left the world of sexual fantasy and began to enjoy the immensely more pleasurable and ecstatic world of true intimacy.

Your Red Light Guy

The Red Light Guy is the guy inside you that you're trying to contact. When you put your hand on your heart, you are reminding that part of you to change its focus from objectifying to admiring. Here are the three basic steps to take:

1. Notice your behavior. Notice the chemical release. Notice that you are objectifying and sexualizing. (Without noticing your behavior, the exercise is useless.)

2. Do something physical. Put your hand on your heart, make a funny noise to yourself, or do the Beard Test.

3. Say your affirmation of a few words or a sentence. This is important. The gist of it is: "I don't want to do what I'm doing now, and this is what I'd like to do instead." Then say thank you.

Opportunities to Use Your Red Light Guy

Henry was driving by a strip club when he saw one of the strippers get out of her car and walk toward a side door. Automatically, he knew he was about to objectify and sexualize. Henry quickly went into his Red Light Guy mode. He touched his chest near his heart and, in the privacy of his car, said aloud to himself, "I don't need to go to this strip club. What I do need to do is go back to work so I can get a good job review."

Gil, a good-looking man in his early thirties, traveled to other states for work. While he was sitting at the hotel bar, an attractive woman started talking to him. Gil was a married guy. He knew what could happen next. It had happened before, and this time he wanted to make a different choice. When the woman turned to the bartender to get another drink, Gil touched the center of his chest, pretending to straighten his tie, and said his Red Light Guy words to himself: "I want to let go of objectifying this woman and be faithful to my wife." It worked.

Reed, a sex addict in recovery who'd been married for six months, was at a restaurant with four of his single guy friends. All of the guys couldn't help noticing the young waitress's healthy cleavage. Reed glanced for an instant and immediately recognized the familiar tingling sensation and release of chemicals into his system. He knew he could start a fantasy about this woman and either try to get her to have sex with him or masturbate later while thinking about her. Reed quickly called on his Red Light Guy, put his hand on his chest, and silently said to himself, "I want to let go of sexualizing and be more available to my beautiful wife."

A word of caution: Many guys think that by using their Red Light Guy and looking away from a great shot of cleavage, they will be missing a thrill and denying themselves a fantasy of having sex with the woman whose cleavage seems so appealing. This is a typical reaction that frequently occurs with men when they're younger and their hormones are raging. But if you're a sex addict, giving in to staring at the cleavage and starting a fantasy can only lead to trouble. If you're married now or engaged, continuing to objectify and escape into fantasy can definitely lead to trouble. Even if you're single, it's really not appropriate to objectify and sexualize. While you fixate on your addiction, you won't be available for a relationship of true intimacy, which is much more satisfying than one based on objectification.

EXERCISE: Put Your Red Light Guy to Work

At least once a day in the coming week, pay attention to when you objectify and sexualize. You could be in a restaurant, in line at the movies, at a store, at work, or just walking down the street. When you become aware of a physical change in your body (maybe a rippling sensation of pleasure starts and chemicals are released that signal the onset of addictive behavior), take your hand and put it on your heart. Avoid doing this when the woman who inspired the feelings can see you. You can be subtle, pretending to check a button on your shirt. Say a positive statement to yourself. It could be one of your own or one of the following:

- "I want to release the energy of objectification, and I'd like the energy that's running now to be turned into something that is useful and positive."

- "I no longer want to objectify and sexualize. I want this energy to be turned to the positive."

- "I want to let go of the objectification energy and be closer to my wife."

- "I want to let go of sexualizing this woman and do something useful and creative."

- "I'd like to let go of feeling that I want to have sex with that woman, and I'd like to be better at my work instead."

- I want to stop objectifying and work on having a relationship with a real woman.

Using your Red Light Guy is not a miracle. It might not work the first time, or the second, or the fifth. But if you keep at it, it *will* work. It's not easy to change your behavior, but you can do it. If you regularly use your Red Light Guy, you will start to realize that you're objectifying less and enjoying life more. Also remember, objectification takes away from your intimate sexuality. When you're not objectifying all the time, when you do have the opportunity to appropriately sexualize, you will have a better time with your partner and a bigger peak experience, and you won't feel ashamed.

In the next chapter, I'll explain a fun technique called "First Thought Wrong," which you can use to help you break the habit of automatically listening to your addict subpersonality.

CHAPTER 12

First Thought Wrong:
Learn Not to Trust the Thoughts of Your Addict

Y ou may have heard of a comedian named Mark Lundholm (marklundholm.com), who specializes in 12-step stand-up comedy. He vacillates between screamingly funny and profoundly serious (but is mostly funny). In telling the story of how he found out he was a sex addict, Lundholm described waking up one morning lying naked, in the fetal position, in front of a porn shop—with a candy cane in his ass! The audience laughed. Many of them were probably thankful that they had not hit that sort of bottom.

Identifying Your Addict's First Thoughts

Lundholm talked about how, when he was in his addictive disease, his thought process was severely flawed. He called this notion "First Thought Wrong." He described that what he meant by First Thought Wrong was that the addict's first thought was usually the wrong thought. You probably know what he meant—and it's no joke.

Part of your thinking process might include First Thought Wrong in general, but it can happen most often when you're in addict mode. Lundholm half-jokingly talked about not trusting any thought, in addictive circumstances, until you get to thought number six or seven. How many thoughts do you have to think during triggering or addictive times before you hit a "right thought"? Here's an example of the addict's thinking process after seeing an attractive woman in a store, workout center, or almost anywhere else on earth. Maybe this is a little bit like your addict talking to you:

Addict: (First thought) I want to have sex with her.

You: Stop thinking that.

Addict: (Second thought) Okay. I just want to look at her and imagine having sex with her.

You: No!

Addict: (Third thought) Okay, okay. I'll just use my X-ray vision to imagine her naked.

You: What? No! Stop! Look away!

You probably get the idea of how this works and how quickly. If this was how you thought and if you practiced the Red Light Guy technique from chapter 11, you could look away, put your hand on your heart, and say whatever words are your cue to stop the process of acting out before it goes too far.

I want you to remember the process of First Thought Wrong. Watch your thinking process. It can actually be amusing (at least sometimes) to notice the mental gymnastics your addict goes through to try to push you toward acting out sexually. First Thought Wrong is another tool to enable you to stop the process of reacting automatically and being triggered by your history. First Thought Wrong could change your life.

Making First Thought Wrong Stick

When I first learned about First Thought Wrong as a recovering sex addict, I took action. I wrote "First Thought Wrong" on sticky notes and put them in my car, on my computer, and on the bathroom mirror. I added a little smiley face under the words to remind myself to see the humor in First Thought Wrong situations. Seeing the notes, I was reminded and I practiced not listening to my first thought, especially if it was the addict's first thought.

Not every single first thought is wrong. If you've been practicing the tools and techniques described in this book, you may see a beautiful woman about to bend over and quickly look away. You know that if you don't look away, your addict may take over. But what if you still automatically look?

If your addict is still in control, your first thought is going to be to keep looking and possibly start a fantasy. When your addiction kicks in, when fear kicks in, when shame kicks in, or when judgment kicks in, it's not going to lead to anything positive. In these situations, your first thought moves you in the direction of your addiction.

Nothing good is going to happen when you give in to your addictive thought pattern. You probably developed this pattern as part of a story that originated in a difficult childhood. But you don't need it anymore. By paying attention and using the technique of First Thought Wrong, you witness yourself thinking, speaking, and acting, and you can recognize your impulses a split second before they actually cause you to act out sexually.

As I practiced First Thought Wrong and kept putting up sticky notes, sometimes others would see the notes and ask me about them. That gave me an opening to tell the story of the comedian Mark Lundholm and First Thought Wrong. By explaining First Thought Wrong to others, I anchored in that this was a very valid way to notice my thinking process. By "anchor in," I mean to do with a thought what you do with a boat—anchor it so the boat can't drift away. When I don't want an addiction-awareness technique I'm using to drift away, I anchor it in. I encourage you to do the same.

One way to anchor in a technique is something I have my counseling clients do. Go ahead and make First Thought Wrong sticky notes to remind yourself to be on the lookout for your first thoughts. Try to remember that disrupting your addict's thought process might not work until you get to the third thought, the fourth thought, or even the seventh thought. And if you keep First Thought Wrong in mind, you have another tool in your recovery tool bag to disrupt the triggering process.

■ Tony's First and Third Thoughts Wrong

Tony had been in counseling for his sexually compulsive behavior for only a short time. One day a woman gave an in-service presentation at the company where Tony worked. Although she dressed in a stylish black business suit, the woman's large breasts were not something she could easily tone down. Tony hardly heard a word of the presentation because his focus was on imagining her breasts.

When it was time for a lunch break, Tony's first thought was that he needed to drive to a strip club. But he had learned the technique of First Thought Wrong, and he quickly stopped himself. His second thought was to realize that visiting a strip club would cost time and money and that he would end up feeling shame. Then his third thought was that he needed to go to a video store and get an X-rated DVD to watch later, or maybe to even start watching on his laptop while in his car. Tony realized that, like his first thought, his third thought was wrong. Again, the addict was pulling him toward acting out.

Tony's fourth thought was, "What else?" What could he do at that moment instead of going to a strip club or buying an X-rated DVD? Now that he had resisted his addict subpersonality, Tony decided to reward himself with an ice cream sundae. Although it wasn't the healthiest choice for lunch, ice cream had been a comforting, fun, and thoroughly enjoyable food choice for him since he was a kid. And he would have time to get to the ice cream parlor and get back to work for the start of the rest of the presentation. Tony used to be chronically late in getting back to the office after lunch. His coworkers knew this and his boss had started to notice. But since he had begun to deal with his sexually compulsive behavior, lateness was rarely an issue. Tony was even in line for a promotion.

Tony could have gone to lunch with some of his coworkers and the woman who had given the presentation. But, even though he'd made a lot of progress in counseling, Tony knew that he wasn't yet at a stage of recovery where he could sit at the same table at a restaurant with the woman and not be triggered by the sight of her.

Tony's entire thought process at the start of the lunch break occurred within a minute. Our thoughts happen quickly and, in an instant, we can embark on a wild ride with our addict. A chemical release can be triggered. The pull toward orgasm can occur. But remembering First Thought Wrong can slow the process down enough for you to make another choice—or even stop the process in its tracks.

■ *Suzy's First Thought Wrong*

Although we've mostly been looking at examples of men with sexually compulsive behavior, I have had a number of women clients. The following example was e-mailed to me from a woman client who was grappling with her First and Second Thought Wrong.

"When I heard from my girlfriend that she had contacted my former lover, the first thing I did was pull him up on the computer. I was ready to send my message to tell him that I was sooo over him and had nothing to do with her contacting him. But I didn't! I waited. My next thought said, "Not a good idea." But I have to admit that somebody inside of me really wants to get in touch with him. I'm just glad that I had the patience to wait out my first thought. I know in my heart that I have to live with his rejection and realize that being with him wasn't right to begin with. The thing I need to get is that, even though he has rejected me, I still have value. That's what I really need to anchor in."

First Thought Wrong and What Else?

In the example with Tony choosing to eat an ice cream sundae, he went through the process of First Thought Wrong and ended up with What Else? The What Else? can be a physical reward, but it doesn't have to be. I encourage my clients to acknowledge their process of overcoming sexually compulsive behavior to at least three trusted people whom they talk to on a regular basis. So, the What Else? could be to talk to others.

If the thought of doing this makes you uncomfortable, you might need to face up to the fact that your secret is likely already out. Even if you haven't directly told these people about your sexual acting out, on some level they probably know. If your wife or girlfriend is one of the people you can talk to regularly, then the odds of her knowing are very high. You could start by telling one or more of these people that you're reading this book and that you need to continue to change and disrupt your addictive-thinking process by using a technique called First Thought Wrong.

You could further explain that, to accomplish First Thought Wrong, you want to be accountable to them, just for your own sake. Let the person know that you're giving them permission to politely ask you, "How are you doing with that First Thought Wrong process?" The reason accountability is important is that your mind will try to trick you into going to the strip club, looking at porn, visiting a massage parlor, or whatever it is you do to act out sexually. Being accountable to others will help to keep you in line with First Thought Wrong and tell your addict-mind that those wrong thoughts are not okay. Knowing that you're accountable for your actions, that you may have to admit how well or poorly you're doing with First Thought Wrong, can help short-circuit the actions that usually follow your wrong thoughts.

Then what do you do? This is where What Else? comes in. Try to choose wise, healthy options, such as calling a friend, taking a drive in the country to look at the leaves, or just being quiet.

After you have some experience watching your thoughts with First Thought Wrong, you may notice that large portions of your thoughts are basically drivel. That's true for all of us. Most of our thoughts are recycled from earlier thoughts and are meaningless. The more you can quiet your mind and move into a state of conscious awareness, the more you will see your thoughts rush by like a river with trash floating in it. In fact, it is more productive to have "quiet mind" than to have addictive thoughts.

■ Ellis and Quick Tick

In addition to circumstances where your thoughts are directly related to seeing a woman and starting to objectify, First Thought Wrong can be used in situations where your first thought is to respond with anger. Many people who act out sexually are triggered when they get angry (at someone else or even themselves), which can lead to the familiar short-term comfort of sexually compulsive behavior.

Ellis grew up with an alcoholic father who would fly off the handle for no apparent reason. The "normal" way of relating in Ellis's family was to shout. As an adult, Ellis unconsciously (and therefore automatically) modeled himself after his father. Ellis was quick to get ticked off, which often led to violent behavior or actions. This, in turn, would prompt Ellis to act out sexually.

As an exercise, Ellis used First Thought Wrong in a dialogue with his angry addict subpersonality, whom Ellis called "Quick Tick."

Ellis: I can't believe she did it again. My wife invited her relatives over this weekend without telling me. Damn her!

Quick Tick's First Thought: You need to do something for yourself. Let's go use the basement computer to watch porn and jack off.

Ellis:	Why do you always come out when something goes wrong, Quick Tick? Why are you always my First Thought Wrong?
Quick Tick:	I'm just trying to help. You'll feel better.
Ellis:	No, that's not true. I won't feel better. Well, maybe for a second—then I'm right back where I started. No, worse. I'll feel ashamed to have slipped up and failed.
Quick Tick:	It's easy for me to get you worked up. I mean, you're already angry most of the time. And when you're angry, I can easily push you to act out. It's great, because when you act out, you end up having even more problems in your relationships. Then you get angry and act out more. It's a perfect system for me.
Ellis:	But not for me! What happens if I refuse to let you in my head and in my heart?
Quick Tick:	I'll push through until I beat you. I will always be your first thought.
Ellis:	No. You're my First Thought Wrong! But, if I observe how you work your way into my head, I can beat you. I can stop you from showing up and causing me pain.
Quick Tick:	Never gonna happen. I'll find a new way to get to you. I am unstoppable. Your dad was like this. His dad was like this. And *you're* like this.

Ellis: No. I now know that you are my First
            Thought Wrong. I don't have to listen. I'm
            not going to listen. I know that if I look at
            my emotions and see how I react to things,
            I can be the one who is control, not you.

Quick Tick: No matter how you try to get around me,
            I'll always be there.

Ellis: Maybe you will always be there, but I'll be
            the one who's in control of the situation,
            not you. I will take a moment to step back
            from the situation and I'll realize that you're
            telling me a First Thought Wrong. If I listen
            to you, I end up pushing people away from
            me. Then I believe that I have to go jack
            off by myself, feeling sad and alone.

Quick Tick: That's who you are.

Ellis: No. That's the story I told myself and that
            you want me to continue to believe. But
            I don't have to listen to you or your First
            Thought Wrong. My second thought can
            be that it's not worth it to me or to those
            around me to immediately jump to anger. I
            don't need to get angry and cope by acting
            out. I can take a deep breath and not
            listen to First Thought Wrong. After that,
            I can ask myself, "What else?" and make a
            positive choice.

EXERCISE: Anchor In First Thought Wrong

Write "First Thought Wrong" on sticky notes and post them where they will be reminders to you. If you don't want this to be too public (at work, for example), put a sticky note on the inside of your wallet. That way, every time you open your wallet you'll see the note, but no one else will.

If you practice First Thought Wrong, along with the other techniques in this book, you can reach a point where you no longer need an addictive coping strategy. Or you might need to use coping strategies less, because your addict mind no longer exerts the pull on you to act out sexually. That may sound impossible now, but it's definitely possible for you to be mostly free of addictive thoughts leading to addictive behavior.

If you continue to listen to your negative thinking, you will most likely have a life of suffering, shame, and pain. Once you no longer instinctively have those thoughts, or you have them but can quickly notice and stop them, you will no longer automatically act out sexually. So start now by creating those sticky notes. And every time you catch sight of one, consider the possibility that you can be free of your addiction.

In the next chapter, you'll move another step closer to the point where you can turn back the tide of negative thinking.

CHAPTER 13

Who's in Charge Here? *Taking a Stand With Your Addict*

This chapter is about getting down and dirty. We're going to be confronting the doubts that your old story might still be throwing up in your face—and I do mean throwing up. It's time to take a stand. It's time to take what you have learned in First Thought Wrong and build on it by using First Thought Wrong along with Taking a Stand.

The Not-So-Silent Retreat

I'm just a regular guy, but somehow I signed up for a silent retreat in Santa Barbara, California. The idea behind this gathering was to remain silent, which meant no talking for any reason. I was to practice this for a whole week to get more in touch with who I am without the distraction of noise and conversation. The trouble was that I'm a person who likes to talk. In fact, I'd never not talked for more than fifteen or twenty minutes, unless I was sleeping. The folks running the silent retreat said that if I wanted to optimize this situation, I shouldn't talk, read a paper, write, or watch TV. I shouldn't do much of anything. Since I'd paid a bunch for this retreat, I decided to get the most out of it. So I stopped talking.

The first night, after I went to sleep in my hotel room, an amazing phenomenon started to happen. I woke up at 2 a.m., apparently "hearing" the inner voice of what I think of as my "false self." Many psychologists have described the *false self* as a personality a child creates to please his or her mother, as opposed to the true personality or true self (Masterson and Lieberman 2004). The false self is a negative subpersonality similar to the subpersonalities I described in earlier chapters.

That night at the silent retreat, my false self's message for me was, "Get the hell out of here! This is ridiculous. It's just a bunch of hippies! You've got a fast car and could be home in four hours. You could just take a week off. Don't tell anyone. You could just go to the movies, ball games, or whatever. Just get out of here—fast!"

I could've jumped out of bed. Instead, I saw this for what it was: First Thought Wrong. I started saying my ABC's over and over. My ABCs was what I had done for years to counter-act thoughts that were disrupting my sleep. After about twenty minutes (and a lot of ABCs), I fell back to sleep.

Like clockwork, at 2 a.m. the next night, the voice in my head started yapping at me like a bull terrier on the attack. After I did the ABCs for fifteen minutes, I was so bored that I fell asleep. It worked, but it was tedious.

On the third day of the retreat, I was starting to notice how nice it was not to talk. My mind was slowing down, and there was less "blah, blah, blah" in my brain. I was surprised to see how pleasant it was to just be still, without all the repetitious mental claptrap that usually annoyed me.

However, that third night I again woke up at precisely 2 a.m. I had left the sliding doors open in my second-floor hotel room. It was late summer and windy out, and there was heat lightning and thunder. Again, the voice in my head started up. "Get out of here. Go home. Leave now." This time, however, without thinking at all, I sat up in bed, raised my hands over my head, and said in a loud voice, "Kill me or shut the fuck up!" I was talking to my addict self—and I meant it. I immediately wrapped my arms around my head because I really was serious about this. It was time to take a stand. I was willing to die from a lightning strike rather than listen to this craziness in my head a moment longer. Suddenly, I fell back and was asleep before my head hit the pillow.

In all the years since that time, I've never woken up with a worry in the night.

By taking a stand, I stood up to my inner voice. From that experience, I knew I could take a stand against any First Thought Wrong, any inner voice, including the voice of my addict. The lesson in my tale of taking a stand against an inner voice at a silent retreat is that you can take a stand, too. You have that power.

Take a Stand with Your Addict's Voice

When you hear your mind going on and on with that stream of nonstop thoughts, you can put your hands over your head and say (to yourself or aloud), "Shut up! I don't want this kind of pain anymore! I won't listen anymore. So just shut up!"

The next day I walked from the silent retreat to a nearby drugstore. I had a paper cut and needed some antibiotic ointment.

After locating the product, I walked up to the cash register and saw the cashier, a stunning, blonde, teenage California girl. To my surprise, she asked if I was a race car driver. When she smiled, I remembered I was wearing a Laguna Seca Race Track hat. I smiled back. Here was my fantasy come true. Although still abiding by the rules of the silent retreat, I desperately wanted to tell this lovely young woman that I was, indeed, a race car driver. I wanted attention from her, even though I was in recovery. I was conflicted. But I just put my hand on my heart and smiled at her. She said, "Oh, you're one of those people from the retreat."

On the walk back to the retreat, I started laughing. I had stood up to my addict's voice and I realized that I was running my life, not my addict. I was glad I had abided by the rules of the retreat and hadn't spoken in the drugstore. I'm a middle-aged man, and I would've said something silly about being a race car driver to get attention from the beautiful teenage cashier.

Is the Tail Wagging Your Dog?

When you listen to your addict subpersonalities, you are letting your addict run your life. As I mentioned in chapter 5, when the tail is wagging the dog, you are not in charge. But you can reframe your basic functioning so that the dog—you—is wagging the tail. You can take charge of your life.

By this point in the book, you probably know how to take charge. You've seen that you have internal subpersonalities, complexes, players in the amphitheater, a story based on your history, and an addict subpersonality who wants to run your life. Maybe you've done some or all of the processes I've introduced, such as dialoging with your addict.

The truth is that you are stronger than your addict. You are stronger than your addiction, which is really nothing more than a coping strategy that most likely began in your childhood. Now that you're an adult, you can choose the standards you want to live by. Do you want to choose the coping strategies of addiction that have let you down so often? Or are you ready to follow new guidelines?

It's time to ask yourself: "Do I want to take charge of my life? Or do I want to keep being that lonely kid who needed to objectify as a way of coping?" Do you want to continue to look at women and pretend you can see through their clothes? Or do you want to look at women and see real human beings with bodily functions, moods, and histories? You know the patterns of your addict—how you feel good for a moment but later feel pain and suffering. Do you want that addict to continue to run your life? Do you want the tail to wag the dog? Or are you ready to step up to the plate and live a healthy, fulfilling life?

■ Steve Takes a Stand—Literally

A counseling client of mine named Steve had a weakness for porn magazines. Although he wasn't into truly hard-core material, he couldn't get enough of softer porn with perfect-looking fantasy women. Steve would search for material online, but he also enjoyed thumbing through magazines. In fact, magazines were how he was first introduced to porn and were still a huge draw for Steve.

After working with me in counseling, Steve had stopped looking at porn. He was making different decisions in his life and felt good about himself. But he was still living in a world where porn was readily available. He adjusted to this fact by having strict guidelines about where he would look when he was on the computer. He also purposely avoided any stores or newsstands where porn magazines might be present.

One afternoon, my office phone rang. I was between sessions and picked up the call. It was Steve, and he was in distress.

"I just saw a porn magazine!" he blurted. "I couldn't help it! It was on the road as I drove by."

Only an addict would notice a porn magazine on the side of the road while he was driving, I thought, amused. Then I had an idea.

"What should I do?" Steve's agitation was palpable. He had worked hard and now felt in danger of slipping.

"Did you stop?" I asked.

"No, I kept driving, then pulled over and called you," he replied. "What should I do?"

"Turn your car around and drive back to where you saw the magazine."

"What?" said Steve. "You want me to go back?"

"Yes. Turn your car around and drive back," I said. "And stay on the phone with me."

Steve drove back to the spot where he had seen the magazine. I told him to turn off the engine and get out of his car. There wasn't a lot of traffic at that time of day, so I told him to walk up to the magazine and, without touching it, tell me what it was.

"It's a Playboy!" he yelled.

This was exactly the type of porn magazine that Steve used to spend hours with. Now he was in a panic.

"Okay," I said. "Piss on the magazine."

"What?" said Steve, astonished. "Right now? What if cars come by, or the police?"

"Just piss on the magazine," I said. "Wait for a time when you don't hear any cars. If the police show up, put them on the phone with me. I'll talk to them."

"Okay," he said, sounding shaky.

"It's time to take a stand," I said.

I heard the sound of his zipper and the sound of a stream hitting the magazine. Then I heard Steve laughing. He was relieved. He had literally taken a stand over the porn magazine and had peed on it. I had him use this as a technique to break up his usual experience with porn. This is similar to techniques I described earlier in the book, like when I went into an adult bookstore with a client, or when a client went into his favorite massage parlor and announced that he would no longer be a customer. If you do something like this, be careful. You don't want to get in trouble.

Since that day, Steve has not had the same compelling desire to look at porn. His experience had shifted. When he even drives near an adult store, he remembers that moment by the side of the road and chuckles to himself.

Taking a Stand with HALT

HALT is an acronym for triggers that can lead you to act out: Hurt, Angry, Lonely, Tired. (The H in HALT can also stand for "Hungry," if eating is part of your acting-out behavior.) When I was part of a 12-step program, HALT was one of the processes we used, and it was a great help to me. In the context of this book, HALT is a combination of noticing your triggers and taking a stand to stop your addict subpersonality from acting out.

First Thought Wrong helps you recognize when your addict is telling you to act out. Next, you can use the acronym, which means to stop: HALT. You can use HALT to remind yourself that you're getting triggered when you feel hurt, angry, lonely, or tired. Saying "HALT" makes you accountable to yourself. You force yourself to stop, even for a second, and consider the consequences. If you are in a location where you can say HALT aloud, it can be a cue to stop yourself from acting out. If you use HALT to stop yourself for even one second, you're giving yourself the opportunity to pause and think of all the agony you've gone through and will continue to go through if you give in to the situations and feelings that are triggering you.

Reward Yourself for Taking a Stand

Almost everyone who successfully breaks the shackles of sexually compulsive behavior has a defining moment of clarity when they realize they are not their addict and are no longer living in reaction to their sexual history. Not all of those moments are as exciting as getting a new boat or a new bike. But almost everybody ends up rewarding themselves with something. What will be your reward? Take a few minutes to make a list of things you've always wanted to do, or have, or experience. Visit a certain place? Spend time with a certain person? Buy a certain thing?

Do you want your relationship to be better? Do you want your career to be better? Do you want to change careers? Now that you're starting the process of being you, you have the opportunity to be better. Maybe you can now have that expensive bicycle, that boat, or that summer home. If you're not acting out and feeling bad about yourself, you will have more time, energy, and willingness to make a better life for yourself. When you're no longer encumbered by negative thoughts, you can be more resourceful than you were before. You may just realize your dream job, start your own business, or have the time to do something beneficial for someone else.

There are no guarantees of what will happen during and after you stop acting out sexually, except that your life will be different. It has to be. You are the one experiencing your life. When you change, your life changes.

Take a Stand and Be Your Own Hero

In my counseling practice, clients frequently send me their dialogues in e-mails. I often just write back with the word "win." Just win. You can win over your addict. You can win over your story. And you can win over your mind. Your mind is promising you this incredible rush, but it's just spinning a story. Or it's promising you an orgasm. But you can have an orgasm with a wonderful person you care about, which is really much better than masturbating alone in a dark room while watching porn.

You will win. You will be your own hero. That's the alternative to staying in the fear, pain, and shame. Maybe you won't have the momentary excitement (after which you feel let down, bad, sad, and alone). But the alternative is that you will always feel better. You will always feel like you. You can be your own hero.

Taking a Stand in the Amphitheater

In this book, I've focused primarily on more general examples of sexually compulsive behavior. However, I've had clients with a very wide range of sexual identities and acting-out behaviors. For instance, Anthony was a good-looking man of average build with brown hair. Growing up, he'd had a conflict-filled relationship with his domineering father. As an adult, he was a chronic overworker. Almost every Friday night, Anthony would go on a "tranny stroll," where he cruised for sexual interactions with transsexuals.

Finally, Anthony used his amphitheater (described in chapter 2) to take a stand with his addict subpersonality.

Anthony:	I'm in the amphitheater.
Anthony's Addict:	It's Friday night, and every Friday night we go out and cruise. So let's get going.

Anthony:	I'm not even gay. Why do you want to be with trannies?
Anthony's Addict:	Well, they know what a man likes. We'll have fun.
Anthony:	But I don't have fun. Sure, it can be exciting and even scary. But the police can pick us up, like we've seen happen with other men.
Anthony's Addict:	You worry too much. We'll have fun.
Anthony:	Those hooker trannies have difficult lives.
Anthony's Addict:	Yeah, but you know how much difficulty we have finding a woman to be with. And the trannies act like they really care about you.
Anthony:	And I never got that from my own father. Is that what this is about?
Anthony's Addict:	No. This is about you getting what you need and having some fun with a man.
Anthony:	No. This time we're not doing it. I'm taking a stand.
Anthony's Addict:	No, you can't. We *have* to do this. We always do this.
Anthony:	Not this time. This time you're going to back off. I've heard enough. This time you're going to shut up and leave me in peace.
Anthony's Addict:	(Silence)

Like Anthony, you can visit your amphitheater and take a stand, no matter what your acting-out behavior is.

In the Octagon: Your Addict Versus Your True-Self

Maybe you've watched Mixed Martial Arts (MMA) cage fighting, in which two men compete in an octagon during five-minute rounds. As in boxing, there are different weight classes. The rules include being able to box, kick, wrestle, and choke. What if it were you and your addict in the ring? It's a fight until one of you wins and, if you don't want to lose, you need to take a stand. The fight might go something like this.

The announcer says, "The gloves are on. In this corner is your True-Self. In the far corner is your Addict-Self. Tonight it's you or him in the octagon. The first round has begun."

Your Addict lands a punch and says, "Let's look at porn. You'll feel so much better."

You land a punch and your Addict staggers backward. You say: "No. We only end up feeling sad and alone."

Your Addict tries to kick you, but you sidestep the kick. Your Addict says, "You're right. Forget the porn. Let's go to that new strip club on the highway. We'll get a lap dance."

You kick back and hit your addict in the shin. "No. We're not going to the strip club on the highway to hell. No lap dances where the woman pretend to like us but see us as pathetic and take our money."

Your addict leaps on your back and gets you in a chokehold. "C'mon. We'll have fun at the strip club. I bet I can get one of the girls to give us a blow job."

Your True-Self breaks the chokehold and tosses your Addict to the mat. "No! You always say that, and it never happens. You just lie. You always lie so we'll do more stupid acting out that only ends up in me feeling bad and losing money. Not this time."

Your addict winces as you twist him into a hold that could break his arm. "All right. I give up!"

The referee declares you the winner. You raise your fists for the crowd. They cheer. You are the hero. Now you notice a woman watching from the side of the ring. Maybe it's your wife or your girlfriend. She smiles and blows you a kiss.

EXERCISE: What Will It Take for You to Take a Stand?

If you've read this far in the book, you probably know too much about yourself to be able to keep making the same excuses about your sexually compulsive behavior. It's similar to that expression about not being able to put the genie back in the bottle. You know how your history created your story, and you've learned techniques of what to do when you're triggered to act out sexually. This exercise is about stepping back and taking a look at where you've been in your life, where you are now, and where you would like to be.

Take five minutes or so to briefly answer the following questions. If you want better results, it would be best to write the answers down:

- In recent years, how has your addiction interfered with your relationship with a current or potential partner? How is your addiction interfering now?

- In recent years, how has your addiction interfered with your work, hobbies, and friendships? How is your addiction interfering now?

- If you take a stand and stop listening to the voice of your addict, how will your life be different in terms of relationships, work, friends, and hobbies?

- What would it take for you to take a stand with your addict and totally stop your sexually compulsive behavior?

- Would you need to be sexually abstinent for a certain period? Would you need to never look at anything resembling porn? Would you need to avoid all situations that might trigger you? How could you do these things?

- If you changed your life, what would it look like?

- When you do take a stand, what are two rewards you could give yourself?

In the next chapter, we will move from taking a stand to "How Good Can You Stand It?"—to realizing that it's possible to take your life to a new level of enjoyment, fulfillment, and prosperity.

CHAPTER 14

How Good Can You Stand It? *Connecting with Yourself and Others*

The conscious and unconscious aspects of mind do a good job of hiding the real you. They continue, at a blistering rate, to spin countless stories to keep you quite diverted. These stories, projections, and memories keep you preoccupied with the past or the future, rather than being in the here and now. A lot of what your mind throws up and at you is based on fear, shame, pain, self-doubt, judgment, and anger. What you're missing is what is happening in each moment. But how do you get in touch and stay in touch with what is happening right now and who you are right now?

Consider this What's Always True statement that I call the magician's secret: there is something beyond your mind that does not change and is always true. That may sound a bit fantastic, but it is, without a doubt, true. As author Eckhart Tolle relates, rather than resisting life as it is in the present moment, you can accept it as it is, without labeling or judgment. This acceptance takes you beyond your mind and your thoughts (Tolle 1999). Tolle often calls the present moment "the Now." The part of you that actually lives in each moment could be called the "Essential Self," "Oceanic Consciousness," "True-Self," or whatever you want. It is the deeper part of you that is always here and isn't compulsive.

Based on my own experience and the experiences of many clients, if you regularly take a few moments to recognize that there is an aspect of you that is always true and always in the moment, you will experience more peace, joy, and serenity. You will start to let go of your fears. You'll become more fearless. The degree that you can accept yourself and "stand" to live a fulfilled existence is one important focus of this chapter. Another way of saying it is: How good can you stand it?

Your Mind Doesn't Give a Damn about You

Your mind has sold you a story about you, and it has been propelling you, in the form of addictive subpersonalities, to carry out its agenda. Do you realize that your mind does not truly care about the real you? It just keeps doing what it has done for years, whether good, bad, or indifferent. Do you think that, if your mind really cared, you would end up feeling shame, pain, and fear?

Most people don't see the bigger picture of their lives. They continue to do the same thing over and over, yet somehow expect their lives to change. I've been urging you to stop operating on automatic. Stop being an automaton. See who you really are and make sure you are living your life in the now rather than living just in reaction to your history.

Remember back in chapter 2 when you turned on the lights in your own private amphitheater? If you practiced that, you probably started to dialogue with one or more addict subpersonalities. Did it sound as if the addict in your mind who was urging you to look at porn and jack off really cared about you? No. More likely, your addict subpersonality was looking for its own version of relief from hurt, anger, or loneliness. Now it's time to move beyond that base-level thinking.

Experiencing Stillness

You've learned how your history led you to create stories on which you've based many of your beliefs and the actions that resulted from those beliefs. This is the soap opera script that has guided your life. You've made decisions based on the rules of your story. Does that story have to do with caring about you? No. But this is your life. You can rewrite your script.

As a start, just put your hand on your heart, close your eyes for a moment, and feel the essence of you. Experience that stillness deep inside yourself. Although this may sound strange, I'd like you to try it anyway. Time and again I've seen the simple act of experiencing stillness lead clients to discover how to live their lives in new and more satisfying ways.

The brief satisfaction you've received from your addictive behavior just doesn't hold a candle to the quiet sweetness and true satisfaction of being your essential self. Again, this may sound spiritual or odd to you. But it's not spiritual, religious, or odd. It's just you truly experiencing (possibly for the first time) who you are beneath all the mind chatter and addictive impulses.

As you stop living in reaction to your story and stop being on automatic, your life will change, most likely for the better. Then the question becomes: How good can you stand it?

Practicing How Good Can You Stand It?

I want you to take a week to do this experiment. For one week, at least twenty-five times a day (make sure you count), ask yourself, "How good can I stand it?" By practicing this technique, you will actually improve each day. Just by asking how good it can be, you'll be ensuring that you'll have a better day and a better week. This question isn't something your mind is used to hearing, and the question itself is the answer, since by asking the question you're actually creating more "good" in your life. If that doesn't make sense, that's okay. This is not a thinking process. You know that what is always true about yourself is your essence. Just as your fingerprint is unique, your essence is your unique fingerprint of your life on this earth. You no longer have to do all this crazy behavior to make you feel happy, comfortable, or wanted. You get to choose now. How good can you stand it?

After you've asked yourself, "How good can I stand it?" twenty-five times a day for a week, ask yourself, "What's always true?" twenty-five times a day. Do this for a week, and don't forget. Keep a note with that question on it in your bathroom, your kitchen, your car, and even in your pocket to remind you. If you actually want change, this is what to do. This practice, which has been in existence for thousands of years, is very strong medicine. I have seen it work with hundreds of individuals. Your reward can be peace, joy, and serenity.

How Intimate Can You Stand It?

When we were growing up, most of us didn't witness much intimacy. Most parents were as loving and kind as they could be, but all too often they were also plagued by neurosis, if not addiction. Many of our parents drank, and some used drugs. We were not taught to be in touch with our essence, and we generally weren't appreciated for who we truly were. In general, our parents had no idea what unconditional acceptance was for themselves or their children. As I've mentioned, it was rare for any child to be given a realistic understanding of sexual behavior.

As you may have already experienced in reading this book, when you try to change, your mind will usually resist. At first, your addict may try even harder to get you to act out. There is often what seems like no end of resistance and sabotage. Even when you see that it's an illusion, your addictive story will try to maintain itself. At this point, I am asking you to observe your behavior and your thoughts as they happen. This is similar to what I do in counseling sessions with clients. You may have experienced this if you've been in therapy.

Typically, when you report a problem, the counselor will ask questions to encourage you to talk more about it. I'm asking you to do this yourself. You can observe your own thoughts and behaviors and train yourself to see problems as they come up. And they *will* come up, all day long. You won't completely get over or remove the story of you, but you will be able to contain it. And that means that you'll be able to say no to porn, to the strip club, to prostitutes, or to whatever it is you've been doing to act out sexually. You must observe yourself and take note of your behavior.

When you're living each day unaware, your story takes over. You automatically live the story all day long and never observe yourself. But this is your life—it's not a dress rehearsal. Your life is flying by, and you are getting older each day. This is your chance to be the person you actually are, rather than an ineffectual version of you living in reaction to your history, your family's problems, or your coping mechanisms.

When you can do this, you are being more intimate with yourself. And when you are intimate with yourself, you can more easily and comfortably experience intimacy with others. You will be able to truly know how deeply rewarding an intimate connection with another human being can be.

■ *Leon's Moment of Stillness*

Leon was a talented and intelligent expert with several university degrees. The only way Leon felt comfortable around a woman was to pay a prostitute. But he wouldn't have sex with her. Instead, he would lie naked next to her while she held him and told him how wonderful he was. He was at the mercy of his stories, which kept him shackled to this sexual compulsion.

In counseling with me, Leon learned about his essential self and being in the moment. As he practiced sinking into the stillness of his essence, his life changed. For the first time, he clearly knew what he wanted, which was to help the world in some way. Shocked by this inner revelation, he called me and told me what had happened. Now what should he do?

I encouraged Leon to contact his network of colleagues, tell them he wanted to change his career path, and ask for any contacts they might have. Before too long, Leon had received a major governmental appointment to travel the world and help hundreds of thousands of people.

This major change in his life began because he took a moment to listen to his stillness. Practicing that exercise over time led to an exponential increase in his How Good Can You Stand It. After a period of dating various women, Leon was able to find true intimacy with a woman, whom he married. At the time of this writing, they live a happy and healthy life with their four children.

■ *Marshall's Moment of Silence*

I remember the day in my office when a client named Marshall sat across from me. He was a young, athletic, accomplished businessman who was motivated to change his life by moving beyond the stories driving his sexually compulsive behavior. I had noticed that he was quite skillful at understanding and practicing what I was teaching him.

"You know, Marshall," I said, "you could do this work." His whole demeanor changed in that moment. Next I said, "Right now, let's just be quiet." Marshall knew what I meant. His eyes teared up, then he closed his eyes and focused inside himself, experiencing that moment of silence.

When he was done, Marshall said, "George, I would like to do this work." I told him that the next step to take was more education. The following day, Marshall enrolled in a degree program for counseling psychology. It took him several years and a lot of work, and now he is a practicing sex-addiction counselor. By helping others, he also continues to help himself maintain a life without sexually compulsive behavior.

Marshall's change didn't occur because I told him he could make more money, which is what often motivates a career change. It was because of that moment of silence. In it, he realized his calling, the desire within him to be and do his very best. For him, that meant counseling work. My point is to encourage you to pay attention to what you're attracted to (besides sex and porn, alcohol or drugs, or material things). What in life would be fun? What would be rewarding? What could you do for eight hours a day without getting bored? Can you feel that place of silence and stillness within yourself and allow it to tell you what might be best for your life?

Can You Stand to Live without Pain and Fear?

If you go into a moment of stillness and find a change in your life that you really desire, your stories may tell you that you're not good enough to do it. You may feel as if you're a fraud or not worthy of getting what you want. These are examples of First Thought Wrong. You are a unique and valid individual. It's just that your mind rarely gives up. There is no magic when you go into essence. Pain and fear will still try to come back and invade your life. Sometimes you don't get anywhere. But if you're diligent about being in touch with your essence in the moment, the degree to which you can "stand" to live a better life will change.

You must be more relentless than your mind and your story. Remember to ask yourself these two questions: "How good can I stand it?" and "What's always true?" Asking these questions can gradually tear down your barriers to change. These questions can help break down your story. You can eventually discover who you really are, what you want to do, which people you want to be with, and possibly even how much money you want to make. It's up to you, and it can start now.

The Moment of Truth

If you practice the techniques and suggestions in this book, you might experience what could be called a moment of truth. This is a decisive moment when you know your addiction is being lifted. When Leon realized he wanted to do work that would benefit the world, he had a moment of truth. When Marshall understood that he wanted to be a sex-addiction counselor, he had a moment of truth. These moments are times of clarity in which individuals frequently move beyond addiction into the truth of who they are and are able to find a new focus for their lives.

My own moment of truth occurred after years of sexually compulsive behavior that had drained me both financially and emotionally. In dialoging with myself, I went into the silence and asked my essence to please help me stop being repeatedly drawn into sexually compulsive behavior. That night I purposely drove to the O'Farrell Theatre in San Francisco, where I'd gone for years. I got out of my car, walked up to the side of the building, and stood in the silence for a few minutes. Then I spit on the building. This may seem strange, or even silly, but it was a ritual that worked. It was one of my moments of truth. After that moment, I no longer had the same thoughts about driving to any adult theater.

I stopped wanting to masturbate while remembering the porn stars I had seen at that theater. My compulsion had been lifted. I was able to focus on how good I could stand my life being, and from that moment on I could only get better. Without needing to focus on the objectification and sexualization fantasies inherent in my addictive behavior, I was eventually able to have a relationship with a real person and experience true intimacy.

In addition, through my own moment of truth and moments of stillness, I was motivated to help others. In doing so, I've been able to teach what I have learned, which has, in turn, continued to help my own recovery. In fact, I took the worst thing that had happened—the addiction that had ruined my life and tortured me every day—and turned it into a thriving business.

My questions for you are "What will you do?" and "What do you want?" In the silence, what does your essential nature tell you to do? And will you have the nerve to go after it? Is it to enroll in school? Is it to make that call to get the job you've always wanted to try? Is it to have the nerve to call the woman who is available and with whom you think you might be able to have an intimate relationship? How good can you stand it?

EXERCISE: A Contract with Yourself

When you are in your place of stillness and you experience who you truly are, there is no addiction. There are no bad feelings in that place of inner quiet that is uniquely yours. In that space, you are at your most expansive and capable. This is when you are most truthful with yourself. This exercise is about allowing yourself the opportunity to experience the clarity of your uniqueness. Doing so will enable that place inside you to provide you with ideas on how to make your life better.

Read through the instructions for the exercise and then take about ten minutes to follow the steps:

1. Put your hand on your heart.

2. Ask yourself, "Addict, are you there?" Wait to see what happens.

3. If your addict makes you feel ashamed, ask Shame, "What do you want?" Take note of the answer. If Shame wants you to feel bad, tell it that you don't need to.

4. If you feel something else, ask that feeling, "What do you want?" Take note of the answer.

5. Ask whatever you are feeling if it's standing in the way of you improving your life. Ask why it's obstructing you.

6. Imagine intimacy. Imagine it in the silence, without the chatter of your negative subpersonalities.

7. Ask your essence about intimacy. That part of you already knows.

8. Imagine that you can stand more intimacy in your life.

9. Ask yourself, "Can I stand to make my life better?"

10. Ask, "What concrete steps do I need to take to increase the chances of improving my life?"

11. Allow yourself to pay attention to your answers, what your mind is saying, what you know to be true, and how good can you stand it.

You will probably start to get answers. If you've been following the exercises in this book, the degree to which you can "stand it" may have increased. In other words, you may now be able to stand more moments of feeling good and less shame and pain in your life.

I encourage you to write down your dialogue. As I mentioned before, when you write something down, it takes on more meaning and importance. It becomes more likely to create change in your life. When you write down your dialogue, pay particular attention to your answer to the question "What concrete steps do I need to take to increase the chances of improving my life?" Next, consider those steps a contract or commitment you're making with yourself to take those steps toward a life of greater fulfillment and intimacy.

In the following chapter, we'll explore the impact of your addiction on your family, loved ones, and those with whom you might want to be intimate.

CHAPTER 15

The Incredible Pleasure of True Intimacy

The sex addict's turn-on is a fantasy based on objectification. Can you open your mind to the possibility that the real excitement in your life can become the beauty of a connection with a loved one? This is a deeper level of beauty and immensely more satisfying than a surface experience. It's a beauty you *can* get enough of, as opposed to objectification, which will always leave you wanting more.

Ultimately, objectification is not rewarding. It has led to where you are now. The life of a sex addict stuck in the shackles of addiction is a life of loneliness, shame, and pain. Can you imagine what it would be like to be in a relationship with a sex addict?

When you want to change your way of relating, the first step is honesty.

What to Tell Your Loved One about Change

You can tell your loved one the truth, but you don't need to go into detail. Many times a woman will want to know specifics. She may just want to be sure that you aren't withholding something. However, hearing the details can result in unnecessary damage. If what you tell her hurts her deeply, she may turn what you say into ammunition against you. If you did things with lovers that you don't do with your wife or girlfriend, that can take the focus away from your attempt to be honest.

It's best to explain in a truthful way that you're going through a learning process. You are sorry for what you have done, and you're glad you are not doing it anymore. You have really appreciated your wife's support and, before this, you didn't know any better. But now you do.

What It's Like to Live with You

Your previous or ongoing behavior isn't going to go away over-night, and it will never be completely forgotten—but it can be forgiven. First, you have to realize that you repeatedly lied. How would you like to live with a liar? Most men wouldn't be able to forgive as easily as many women can. Imagine that she was the sex addict, lost in porn and generally out of touch with you. Could you trust her?

Imagine what it would be like to learn that your wife was masturbating to men with giant penises, or she was in chat rooms with men who wanted to tie her up and ravish her. Put yourself in her position and feel, just for a second, how you would feel. What if she were spending hundreds of dollars a month on porn or prostitutes?

Imagine your wife was paying handsome, young men to have sex with her. How do you compete with that? What do you do? That's what it might be like to live with you. It would mean living with fear and pain. A woman in this situation may doubt herself and doubt her femininity. Her sexuality may even be completely compromised.

The rest of this chapter describes ways to relate with loved ones once you've decided to stop your sexually compulsive behavior and start on a course of recovery.

You Feel Triggered—and You're with Your Wife

Several years ago, I was driving while my wife, Paldrom, was in the passenger's seat of my Infiniti. We were on Route 50, leaving Sacramento, California. It was around eight o'clock at night on the dimly lit highway, which made it difficult to see clearly what was on either side of the road. But I was getting triggered. I knew because I felt what I call the "Magic Fingers," which is a feeling of energy moving down my body in a small rush. Paldrom and I had established a relationship based in honesty, so I felt comfortable telling her what was happening.

"I'm feeling kind of sexualized right now," I said. "It's odd."

"What do you think it is?" she asked.

"I don't know," I said, "but the sensation is getting stronger."

By describing my experience to her, I stayed in the moment rather than going into a fantasy. We kept talking, which helped me stay focused as I stared at the mostly empty road ahead.

A few minutes later, on the right, I saw a big sign for an old, familiar strip club. My conscious mind had forgotten that there was a big sign for the club, but my unconscious mind, where the addict likes to lurk and exert its pull, hadn't forgotten for a second. The addict knew the sign was there and was being triggered before I even saw it. This time, when I saw the sign, I started laughing.

I was at a point in my recovery when I would no longer be pulled to act out sexually. Now the trick my mind was playing was just plain funny. Because I'd been open and honest and talked with my wife about what was happening, I was able to discharge the Magic Fingers energy. I wasn't frustrated or angry. It just struck me as very funny.

As we passed the sign for the club, I said to my wife, "Wow! A strip club! I bet you'd like to stop there!"

It was, of course, absurd that she would go to a strip club. That's not something she would ever do. So it was funny. She understood, and we both started laughing. Just joking with her shifted the entire compulsive feeling I'd been having. The mere thought of her being in a strip club with me was enough to wreck my addict subpersonality's negative pull. It was as if a bubble had burst.

Shift Your Triggers from Destructive to Instructive

If you have an experience similar to the one I just described, let it be instructive rather than destructive. Whether you're driving in the car with your wife or sitting on the couch with your long-time girlfriend watching TV, try being honest. Notice when you're getting triggered and share the experience, as long as you're comfortable doing so. Many addicts don't stay connected with others. They go through the motions at their jobs, their hobbies, and their relationships. If you can cultivate at least one honest connection (which could be with your wife, if you're married), you'll find that it's easier to stay connected to others in general, as well as to yourself.

Sometimes just joking about being triggered and sharing that with your wife or significant other can be enough to shift what happens inside you. The next time you get triggered by a similar event, you might smile and say to yourself, "No, not this time."

You can also do this if you are triggered and alone. You can imagine that your wife or girlfriend is there. Or you could, for example, use an imaginary figure such as the phantom mother-in-law or drill sergeant. The goal is to break the addict subpersonality's hold over you. By saying, "No, not this time," you change your Blue Sky and High Heels situation so it no longer has the same power to trigger you.

A side benefit is that, with every step you take to be free of the negative, you are freeing up more energy to be used in a positive way. Another way of explaining this is that the addict's activity is not being taken away and replaced with nothing—something better fills the void. I've had clients go through the recovery process and then have a great idea for a new business or a fantastic hobby. Most of them move on to find a real live partner and have a relationship based on true intimacy. Many good things happen when you change your sexual thought process from negative to positive.

Turn Your Trigger Moments into Relationship Plus Points

As you know, you could get triggered at any time or in any place. Your wife could get a Victoria's Secret catalog in the mail. Your daughter has girlfriends over, and you might get some kind of a hit (what I call the "cheerleaders syndrome"). What happened to me while I was driving in the car with my wife was a Blue Sky and High Heels experience that might also be called "the strip club jitters." You just don't know when you might get an addictive hit.

I've had clients who have reported that they get irritable with the strip club jitters when they drive by (or are even in the general area of) a familiar strip club. They're especially vulnerable to this when a wife or girlfriend is in the car with them. The wife may ask, "What's wrong? What's going on?" But the guy won't talk. Even if he knows what's triggering him, he's reluctant to admit it. He doesn't want to tell her that they're driving by or near a location where he went to a strip club or a porn shop or where he picked up a prostitute. He's afraid that if he says anything at all, his wife will think that he's still acting out sexually, even if he's not.

If this happens to you, you might want to take a moment to simply notice what you're feeling. If you've never talked to your significant other while you were having an impulse, maybe it's best not to bring it up in the moment. Your goal isn't to make her uncomfortable with your honest admissions. What you can do is realize that you want to be open and honest with your wife. You know that honesty will bring you closer. Later, when you're at home, you might explain the situation to her. You could say that, sometimes when you're in the car together, you have sensations or feelings which signal that you're starting to get triggered. You want to be able to talk with her at the time these instances occur. Explain further that talking about the experience of being triggered can help you to break free of the impulses. Ask her if she's willing to help you in this way. If she is, explain that when it happens again, you'll be letting her know. You can further reassure her (and yourself) by letting her know that sharing with her in this way can help increase the level of intimacy in your relationship. You might even have a laugh about it.

One way of explaining your experience to your wife is, "I just got a small trigger. I used to act on it, but I don't anymore." By explaining how you still get triggered even though you've stopped acting on it, you are taking a negative and turning it into a positive. I like to think of the positive benefits you get from this kind of turnaround as *plus points* for a relationship. You're talking about how you experience the triggering process in the context of recovery rather than as a problem. Again, this can increase the level of intimacy in your relationship. Also, if your wife realizes that you are catching your impulses rather than acting out, she will probably be more likely to feel comfortable talking with you. Remember, women have impulses too. Yet, in most cases, they are less likely than men to act out.

When You Take a Startle

While some triggers occur as the result of a prior sexual experience, there may be times when you will have an experience that I call *taking a startle*. For example, you walk into a restaurant with your wife or girlfriend and a young hostess in a low-cut top smiles at you. The take-a-startle moment is when you're about to go into sexualization mode, perhaps imagining the hostess naked or yourself having sex with her. You might remember First Thought Wrong, since your initial thought about her even wanting to have sex with you is probably a wild fantasy.

You can stop yourself by putting your hand on your heart, or whatever method you use to change the situation before you're further triggered. That's when you say to yourself, "No, I don't do that." When you're with your wife or girlfriend and you quickly cut off the triggering process, it becomes a moment that you can celebrate your success. Also, it's best if you can be truthful with your partner while your triggering is happening. If you wait until it's over, your partner may consider you less than truthful.

When I'm seated in a restaurant with my wife, she will notice when I take a startle. My face might twitch for a second and my hand will go to my heart. "Who is it?" she might ask. We'll look around the room and my wife will usually see the woman in question. Because we share the moment, it's not serious anymore. In fact, it can become a moment when you share a smile or a laugh with your wife or significant other.

At a Party with Your Loved One

Eventually, you might have an experience similar to that of an alcoholic who has stopped drinking and goes to a party with his wife. Across the room, they see a middle-aged man who has had too much to drink and is making an ass of himself by flirting with the eighteen-year-old daughter of their host. The young woman is clearly bored and desperately wants to escape from the drunken lecher. Your wife might squeeze your hand. You both smile, knowing that the guy making an ass of himself could be you—but it's not. This moment brings home to each of you the fact that you're *not* acting out—that you've changed. Instead of acting out, you are experiencing a moment of intimacy with your wife.

Triggered at the Movies

Have you ever gone to an R-rated movie and gotten triggered? You leave the theater, start to objectify women, and then think about how you can get time later to masturbate after your wife goes to sleep. That could be the exact moment when you need to say to your wife, "That movie was kind of a turn-on, don't you think?" She might reply, "Yes, it was." Or, "I just thought it was romantic." The point is that you have shared with her how you're feeling rather than emotionally distancing yourself from her and, instead, focusing on sexualizing some other woman. If you *do* start fantasizing about another woman, or the woman in the movie, and you think your wife doesn't notice, then you're in a bigger fantasy than you thought.

You Only Think You're Getting Away with It

A counseling client once described what he thought of as his standard joke. He would sit in his favorite living-room recliner, hold the remote control, and push the channel button, saying to himself, "Come on, *Baywatch*. Come on, *Baywatch*." He would stop only when he saw a rerun of the nineties TV show, which featured buxom blondes in swimsuits. However, his wife knew exactly what he was doing and she would go crazy. He thought this behavior was a laugh. She did not. The moral of this story is that, even if you think you're getting away with something, there is a good chance that you're not.

After several months of counseling, whenever *Baywatch* Guy started to change channels, he would put his hand on his heart and remind himself what mattered to him. He had a personal affirmation that he would say to himself: "I want to watch TV, have a good time, and not sexualize any of the women I see." He would do this even when his wife was present. Obviously, his relationship with his wife improved.

Perhaps you are changing channels in search of cleavage, or perhaps you're surfing for a Victoria's Secret ad. Regardless of the specifics, the person living with you may very well know that you're up to something. The same logic applies when you think you're getting away with scanning women in the mall and imagining them naked, or even looking a little too long at your wife's sister's backside as she walks away.

Similar to the alcoholic who believes no one can tell that he or she has been drinking, you may think you can objectify and no one will be the wiser. Besides your behavior having a negative impact on you, it can also negatively impact those around you. It's time to stop living in a world of denial and delusion.

From Sex Addiction to Intimacy

Sex addiction has no upper age limit, and it's never too late to change. I saw a client in his eighties who had memory loss. If we had a session scheduled, Carl would sometimes make it to my office and at other times end up somewhere else by mistake. Carl's wife loved him and was adjusting to Carl's loss of memory. Carl worked hard at his recovery, which was to not use porn. However, when I encouraged him to do repetitious exercises, he often forgot to do them.

After some trial and error, I assigned him the task of sitting in a room with his wife. They were to sit silently, each thinking about what they wanted most from their relationship. When they came out of that silence, which was to be about a minute, they would each express what they'd been thinking about. They did the exercise and each expressed a desire to renew their intimate connection.

As a follow-up to this exercise, Carl and his wife developed a daily routine. At night, before dinner, she put her hands on the table. Carl covered her hands with his hands and said something nice and loving to her. His words were usually about letting go of addiction and being open to loving her as fully as possible. Next, they switched places so that her hands were on top of his. She told him something nice and loving, too.

What resulted from their mutual minute of stillness and silence was a simple act of intimacy that brought these two loved ones closer together. Take a moment to think about what daily ritual you could do with a loved one that would result in increased connection and intimacy. Then take a risk and tell your loved one about the step you want to take with her.

Your Problem Is Her Problem

When couples are in counseling with me, the woman often wants the man to be the only problem. I tell them both that I am talking to a couple, and the patient is the couple. I want the wife to talk about her issues relating to sex addiction and her life. What does sex mean to her?' Was she betrayed? Abandoned? Physically or sexually abused as a child? Raped as an adult? Although there is no excuse for his behavior, her history will have a bearing on the signals she conveys to the man and what he might do in response.

In many couples, the early excitement of the relationship (frequently based on appearances) soon gives way to reality. If the man wants to continue a relationship of objectification, he may look elsewhere. I encourage both partners to move from objectification of the other to seeing the true beauty of the other person, whether that beauty is inside or on the surface.

It's possible to shift from relating to and even desiring the outward appearance of the person—the objectification—to the true beauty of the person. As I mentioned earlier, you'll be involved with a deeper level of beauty that is immensely more satisfying than a surface experience. It is a beauty you *can* get enough of, that truly satisfies you. With objectification, you will never get enough and will always want more. Ultimately, objectification is both unsatisfying and unrewarding.

A woman may have her own version of objectification. Perhaps she had hopes and dreams that were not fulfilled, of what her man would become and how he would relate to her. Perhaps she was first attracted by his looks or his charm, neither of which lasts forever. Perhaps she is living with disappointment rather than accepting the reality for what it is and the man for who he is. The point is for both you and your partner to move beyond any fantasies of how you would like each other to be and to live in the truth of who you both are. That is where ultimate beauty is found.

EXERCISE: A Step a Day Toward Intimacy

This exercise can increase both your honesty and your intimacy. Explain to your loved one that you want to get in the habit of being completely honest with her. If you get the sense that your loved one is resistant to your honesty, be sensitive to that. Ask her if she might need a therapist, clergyman, or other third party present to help her feel more comfortable. It doesn't matter if she reciprocates and decides to be completely open with you. If she does want to, you can welcome her honesty. But the main point of this exercise is for you to be honest with her. Remember, being honest with her means taking responsibility for your feelings, rather than shaming and blaming. You need to do the following for at least one week:

1. In the evening or near the end of every day, sit down with your wife or loved one.

2. Be completely honest with her about any kind of abnormal thinking you had during that day.

3. You might want to go through your day and relate anything you were ashamed of thinking. You don't have to restrict yourself to thoughts about sex, because sex addiction is not just about sex. It's about self-esteem and how you view yourself and your stories.

Again, if your wife reciprocates, it could bring you closer. But don't pressure her. If she does reciprocate, she also needs to avoid shaming and blaming. However, she doesn't have to say a word. This exercise is about you being honest with people who are close to you. If you are open and honest, your wife is more likely to respond with loving-kindness. If you are vulnerable, you invite vulnerability.

In the next and final chapter, you will learn how to help others while helping yourself.

CHAPTER 16

Tell the Young Men

Many years ago, a very successful businessman with the appearance of a distinguished grey-haired banker began to see me for counseling. Although in his late sixties, Warren had never been married and had actually never had sex with a woman over twenty-five. He had had a difficult childhood and, as an adult, had coped by frequenting adult theaters, where he would masturbate or have sex with the young dancers.

Warren wanted to stop, but he had never known how to change. The prospect of an intimate relationship with a real woman was foreign to him. As he described his sexually compulsive habit, Warren began to sob. "Tell the young men," he said. "Tell them that if they don't stop doing this shit, they'll end up as lonely old men in a dark room with their dick in their hands. Tell them, George."

That's where the phrase I pass along to many of my clients originated. I "tell the young men" the story of Warren, and each one quickly gets the idea that he could easily end up sad and alone in a dark room. My former clients who call or e-mail will often mention that the story of Warren was inspirational to them. They tell me that they don't want to end up that way.

■ *Craig and His Son*

Chapter 6 had an example of Craig, who had fantasized about having a stable or harem of women. In counseling, he had worked to get beyond the fantasy and was finally able to enjoy an intimate and sexual connection with his wife. Craig continued to have counseling sessions and one afternoon, as he sat down across from me, his eyes welled up with tears. I asked Craig why he was upset.

"I was on my computer, checking the browser history," he replied, "and I noticed that my eleven-year-old son had been visiting porn sites." Using a tissue to wipe away a tear, he added, "What do I do?"

"This is wonderful," I told him.

He looked at me as if his counselor had gone bonkers. "Wonderful? What're you talking about?! It's not wonderful."

"Your son was going to do this anyway, right?" I asked.

Craig thought for a moment and nodded. "Yeah, of course he would. Most boys would."

"Okay," I said. "Now it's time to teach him what you most need to learn."

I further explained that one way Craig could strengthen his own resolve not to act out sexually was for him to teach his son, through positive reinforcement, what not to do. Many fathers or mothers would yell at their sons or add blocking software to the computer. A few would even try to have a talk about real intimacy between a man and a woman, as if it were something they actually knew how to practice with their own wives.

"You may not yet have perfect intimacy with your wife," I said to Craig, "but you know enough to explain some things to your son. You can explain the difference between real intimacy with a woman and the masturbatory fantasy of ejaculating onto some fantasy woman's chest or face, which is what he could've seen on the porn sites. You can let him know that, when he's older, real intimacy can be truly satisfying. But with porn, he can never get enough of a fantasy that won't satisfy him."

Craig nodded. He understood what I was saying. It would take some courage to have this talk with his son, but we both knew he could do it. Unfortunately, most parents never have "the talk" with their children. Craig began to see that what had happened had presented him with a wonderful opportunity.

"Remember when you and I talked about how you built your story based on your history?" I asked.

"But," Craig responded, "maybe if I don't say anything, he'll just stop."

"Your son is building his story," I said. "And you have an opportunity to influence him to create a positive story about sexuality. Or you can ignore his behavior and say, 'He's just a boy.' But if you do ignore it, he'll probably just keep looking at porn and recreate the same story about sexuality that you did."

Craig got the point, and he had more than one talk with his son. The son felt his dad was talking to him man to man. This led to a stronger bond between the two of them.

If you have children, your behaviors and beliefs in all areas can have a positive or negative impact on them. If you continue to act out sexually, even if you think you're hiding it, your children can pick up your values and views on sexuality. That process could be subtle or it could be more obvious.

Maybe your son or daughter will catch you going online or hear your wife screaming at you about your addiction. Remember, your children are in the process of building their own stories about life and sexuality. If you don't want them to suffer as you have, be responsible and do not pretend that your acting-out behavior has no impact on your family.

Never Forget That You Are Not Your Story

By this point in reading this book, you understand that the mind fabricates stories as a coping mechanism. What you can accomplish without the stories is usually an extraordinary experience. But getting free of your stories isn't without pain. You may have sleepless nights, wrestling with yourself, thinking you should do porn, find a prostitute, go to a strip club or a massage parlor, or whatever. But if you persuade yourself to use the tools you've learned in this book, and use them every day, your mind can start to change. As it does, you will need to resort to old coping strategies less and you will continue to free yourself of shame, fear, and pain.

In fact, once you've read this book and practiced some of the techniques and exercises, your compulsive urges will never be the same. You know too much now. Maybe you slipped and looked at porn or masturbated while objectifying the weather woman on Channel 3. When this happens, it might look like you're right back where you were—but you're not. You have internalized this work, and it is still with you. What your mind will try to do is to get you to completely forget that you learned anything. "Don't you remember," your mind might say, "we had such a good time?" But you know that's not true. It might have felt good for a moment, but then it was bad, or your wife left you, or you were chronically late for work and missed deadlines.

The good news is that if you follow the techniques and exercises in this book, you can stop a lot of your negative stories and be more in the now. It's very important that you notice when you are objectifying or sexualizing. It's also vital to stop for just a few seconds and let your essence filter those objectifying thoughts or the voice that wants you to act out.

You must be more relentless than your story.

Counteracting your addict's voice is a positive action that can help your mind to change. If you just read this book without taking action, your mind won't necessarily change. Again, you need to take positive actions. Otherwise, the addict subpersonality in your mind will win, convincing you that this is all bull and you need to keep doing the behaviors that have gotten you nowhere.

A Slip Does Not Need to Become a Slide

If you slip, your addict may tell you to just keep going: "Since you've already slipped, you might as well do more." But if you start to slip, or you do slip, that doesn't mean you need to continue to slide. What if you were on a mountainside and you slipped? Would you give up and just keep sliding until you fell off the mountain? Or would you try to get a foothold and keep climbing upward? If you slip in your recovery, you can still stop right there and just keep climbing. You might have some ground to make up, but you can do it. You have the tools.

A crisis can be a gold mine. That may sound contradictory, but it's true. For example, if you're triggered and you successfully resist, you will less likely to be triggered next time. We all live in worlds of chaos and unpredictable moments. When you are prepared, you can turn what could have been a slip into another positive step in your recovery.

■ *From Field Glasses to Hacky Sacks*

When I first moved into my counseling offices, I experienced a possible slip turning into a positive step. There was a high school nearby, and I could see the athletic fields from my office window. I glanced out the window and saw the girls' soccer team running in rows of two, doing a sidestep, and continuing to run. Immediately, my usually quiet addict subpersonality went into cheerleader-alert mode. "We're in luck with this office view," said my addict subpersonality. "Now all we need to do is remember to bring field glasses to work. Imagine the view then!" "No," I said to my addict subpersonality. "No field glasses!"

At that point in my recovery, it was relatively easy for me to say no to my addict subpersonality. But I wanted to go further than that. So I asked myself, "What else? What else can I do?" I immediately drove to a sporting goods store and asked the sales clerk what to buy for a girls' soccer team. The sales clerk suggested those small sand-filled Hacky Sacks that kids like to toss around.

Later that day, I walked onto the practice field adjacent to my office. I felt like a mature adult. I found the girls' soccer coach and presented him with a case of Hacky Sacks for the team. The coach handed out the Hacky Sacks and the girls excitedly began kicking them into the air. As I stood there watching, I could see that these were just normal girls, some of them with pimples, some of them with braces on their teeth, and others just giggling like the kids they were. The point is that I saw them as real people. I had ceased objectifying. I had taken action and gone past the cheerleader syndrome.

■ Simon Tells the Young Men

Fifty-year-old Simon was married and the owner of a high-end auto dealership. He used to have a weakness for topless bars. In counseling, he had learned techniques such as First Thought Wrong and Red Light Guy to stop any negative impulses in their tracks. Simon wanted to acknowledge a good sales month with his sales team. The problem was that these were younger guys who wanted to celebrate by going to a topless bar.

Although Simon may have been able to go to a topless bar and resist acting out sexually (for example, by then visiting a prostitute), he knew that some of these younger guys could develop the same sexually compulsive behaviors that he used to have. Simon also knew that if he went to the club with the young guys, the nineteen-year-old girls giving out lap dances would gravitate to him. They would sense that Simon was the boss and the one with the most money. That would take even more resisting on Simon's part. What could he do?

Simon decided to treat his sales guys to an incredible dinner at an amazing steakhouse. During the dinner, he would explain to them why he chose the restaurant rather than the topless bar. He would "tell the young men" about his addiction and offer his help and support should any of them want or need it. This plan worked well for Simon, and in the following weeks, several of his salespeople spoke privately to him about their own issues with sex addiction.

There will be times when you're with another man or men, and the "we're just being guys" attitude will pervade your interaction. If you don't share the joke about wanting to have sex with the woman with big breasts, it may seem as if you're not being a man. The truth is that those guys are stuck in their child stories of objectifying women while you are being an adult man. Real, grown-up men learn not to treat women as objects.

What to Say to a Possible Sex Addict

I'm not saying that you need to search out people with possible sex addictions who might need your help. But it would be helpful for you to be aware if there is someone in your life who could possibly need help in this area. It might be a friend, relative, or colleague from work who might say, "Can I tell you something in confidence? I seem to have a problem with porn and I can't stop." That person is asking for help.

You may have a friend or a colleague at work who you know is lost in sexually compulsive behavior. Because you have acted out sexually in the past, you may recognize the signs. You now know that this person is in danger of losing his family or job, or both. If it feels right, you can gently approach this person. Remember, it's not your job to help others. However, there is no shortage of people in need of help and, if you want to learn more about your own sexually compulsive behavior, a great way to do that is by teaching others what you've learned.

If you do approach such a person, do not be judgmental. The fact that you've been able to stop your sexually compulsive behavior doesn't give you the right to judge others. In an effort to help, you can offer your own experience. Often, the other person will instantly refuse any help and claim that he doesn't have a problem. In that case, you don't need to go further. On the other hand, if the person responds, "You suffered from that?" then you have an opening.

Let's say that you know your brother-in-law is using porn and that your sister is getting ready to leave him. If you feel nervy, you could take him aside and explain that you know something about sexually compulsive behavior because you've gone through it. If you share a confidence, the other person may be more likely to open up. That is the person to help.

When you do have an opening, you need to be careful to tell the person only what he can handle. For example, you could ask about his history. Then you can bring up the idea of his history leading him to create sexual stories that aren't necessarily true. If he doesn't understand or is unwilling to hear what you're saying, don't try to bombard or berate him. If the person is receptive, you might tell him how you dialogue with your addict, and then share a few insights you've gained through using this technique.

In subsequent conversations, assuming the person continues to show an interest in what you're saying, you could briefly describe a few techniques he could practice to get started. For example, when triggered, the person could put a hand on his heart and say, "I do not need to act out. I want to have a positive relationship with my wife." Of course, he would have his own version, in his own words.

You could explain What Else? When the person is triggered, he could ask himself what else he can do besides act out sexually, which would lead to shame and pain. If you have more discussions with this person, you might explain additional techniques such as First Thought Wrong, Blue Sky and High Heels, and Red Light Guy.

It's important to remember that you are not the person's therapist or counselor. You are talking as a friend. Let me repeat: do not judge. Maybe you're no longer acting out sexually and you feel proud or even arrogant about it. It does not help another person if you talk down to them. Instead, this interaction is about explaining what worked for you. If the person is open to suggestions, he will tell you. If not, you can let it go. In my experience, the other person will say, "Tell me more" about 50 percent of the time. Another 25 percent may call next week and ask to hear more. The other 25 percent don't want help. They may come around at a later date and seek help from you or others. Or they may end up being miserable, getting divorced, or losing their jobs. But you can't help someone who has no interest in changing.

The person who is receptive will give you cues regarding what he needs to hear next to be helpful with his particular situation. If Red Light Guy is needed, you tell him that one. If he says, "Oh, it came out of nowhere," you can explain Blue Skies and High Heels. If he's walking around a mall every day just to look at women, describe how you do the Beard Test and don't need to look twice at a woman. If another man belittles you for not sexualizing women, it could lead to an opening for you to describe how amazing it is to have real intimacy with your wife or girl-friend—and how the sex is better and more fulfilling that you ever imagined possible.

Whether or not the other person follows up on what you're saying, by trying to help others you remind yourself of what you've read in this book and of all your own accomplishments.

EXERCISE: Help Two People

Your last assignment is to help two people you think might be acting out sexually. By doing this, you will also be helping your-self. In fact, what you can pass on to others could be the most important technique this book has to offer. If you remember any-thing from this book, remember What Else? "What else can I do right now instead of acting out?"

When you're describing this technique, tell those you're helping to just start practicing. Just start saying it. Let them know not to wait until they want to act out. They should try saying it when they're not triggered so they'll be ready. Explain that when they're seized by the impulse to act out, they may not have time to think. But if they start practicing now, they will remember. It may not work the first time, or the fifth time, but it will eventually work to think to themselves, "What else can I do besides act out?" Can they play some pool? Watch TV? Eat candy? What else can they do that won't destroy their life?

If there is only one thing you can take away from this book and share with others, it's this idea of What Else? By using it, the sex addict gives himself choices. Remember, your mind is entrenched and your story did not start last year. It started when you were young. But you can change. If you tell yourself you can't, that's your story—your mind—talking. If someone else tells you they can't change, then that's their mind talking. Remember, there is a part of you inside who does not need to listen to your addict subpersonalities. There is an essence of you who can take a stand and say, "What else?" Go ahead. Say it. Start right now. Say, "What else?" Then help two others.

And help yourself in the process.

References

Adams, K. and P. Carnes. 2002. *Clinical Management of Sex Addiction*. London: Psychology Press.

Assagioli, R. 1965. *Psychosynthesis: A Manual of Principles and Techniques*. New York: Viking Press.

Carnes, P. 2001. *Out of the Shadows: Understanding Sexual Addiction*. Center City, MN: Hazelden.

Carnes, P. 2011. "Important Definitions," *Sexhelp.com*. http://www. sexhelp.com/addiction_definitions.cfm.

Dayton, T. 2000. *Trauma and Addiction: Ending the Cycle of Pain Through Emotional Literacy*. Deerfield Beach, Florida: HCI Books.

Engel, B. 2010. *Healing Your Emotional Self: A Powerful Program to Help You Raise Your Self-Esteem, Quiet Your Inner Critic, and Overcome Your Shame*. New York: John Wiley and Sons.

Fairbairn, R., D. W. Winnicott, H. Guntrip, and P. Gray. 2006. *Psychology*. New York: Macmillan.

Gray, P. 2006. *Psychology*, 5th ed. New York: Worth Publishers.

Hamilton, N. Gregory. *Self and Others: Object Relations Theory in Practice*. 1990. North Vale, NJ, and London: Jason Aronson, Inc.

Herek, G., J. Cogan, J. Gills, E. Glunt. 1997. Correlates of internalized homophobia in a community sample of lesbians and gay men. *Journal of the Gay and Lesbian Medical Association* 2: 17-25.

Katehakis, A. 2010. *Erotic Intelligence: Igniting Hot, Healthy Sex While in Recovery from Sex Addiction*. Deerfield Beach, Florida: HCI Books.

Knauer, S. 2002. *Recovering from Sexual Abuse, Addictions, and Compulsive Behaviors*. New York: The Haworth Press, Inc.

Levine, P. and M. Kline. 2007. *Trauma Through a Child's Eyes: Awakening the Ordinary Miracle of Healing*. Berkeley, CA: North Atlantic Books.

Love, P. and J. Robinson. 1990. *The Emotional Incest Syndrome: What to Do When a Parent's Love Rules Your Life*. New York, N.Y.: Bantam Books.

Masterson, J., A. Lieberman. 2004. *A Therapist's Guide to the Personality Disorders: The Masterson Approach*. Phoenix, AZ: Zeig, Tucker & Theisen, Inc.

Rawson, R. and R. Urban. 2000. *Treatment for Stimulant Use Disorders*. Upland, PA: Diane Publishing.

Ronen, T. and A. Freeman. 2006. *Cognitive Behavior Therapy in Clinical Social Work Practice*. New York, N.Y.: Springer Publishing.

Sinetar, Marsha. 1989. *Do What You Love, The Money Will Follow: Discovering Your Right Livelihood*. New York: Dell.

Tolle, E. 1999. *The Power of Now: A Guide to Spiritual Enlightenment.* Novato, CA: New World Library.

Wilber, K., J. Engler, and D. Brown. 1986. *Transformations of Consciousness: Conventional and Contemplative Perspectives on Development.* Boston: Shambala.

George N. Collins, MA, is founder and director of Compulsion Solutions, an outpatient counseling service in the San Francisco Bay Area specializing in the treatment of sexually compulsive behavior. A former sex addict himself, Collins is a professional member of the Society for the Advancement of Sexual Health and is recognized as an expert on sexually compulsive behavior. Visit him online at www.compulsionsolutions.com.

Andrew Adleman, MA, is a writer and book editor in the greater Los Angeles area. He has also worked in the movie industry and as a psychotherapist.

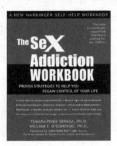
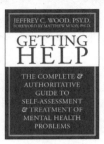
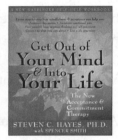

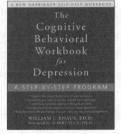